Intricately Woven:
Life/Work Direction's Story

Eunice Russell Schatz

xulon PRESS

Copyright © 2011 by Eunice Russell Schatz

Intricately Woven: Life/Work Direction's Story
by Eunice Russell Schatz

Printed in the United States of America

ISBN 9781609576660

All rights reserved solely by the author. The author guarantees all contents are original and do not infringe upon the legal rights of any other person or work. No part of this book may be reproduced in any form without the permission of the author. The views expressed in this book are not necessarily those of the publisher.

Unless otherwise indicated, Bible quotations are taken from the New Revised Standard version. Copyright © 1989 by the Division of Christian Education of the National Council of Churches of Christ in the U.S.A. Used by permission. All rights reserved.

Photos on pages 35, 98, 118 and 138 by Dorothy Greco.

www.xulonpress.com

for
RICHARD B. FAXON

*whose charismatic presence and vision
prepared the way for the formation of
Life/Work Direction
and whose faithful ministry
enriched the lives of all he touched.*

Table of Contents

Introduction

Prologue 1

Part One: Letting Life Reveal A Calling: *seeing the pattern in the strands of life story* 3

> CHAPTER 1
> In the Beginning: *two colors appear* 5
>
> CHAPTER 2
> Endings: *letting go of some strands* 9
>
> CHAPTER 3
> The End of Ideals: *when the colors fade* 15
>
> CHAPTER 4
> How a Calling is Shaped: *tracing the origins of the design* 25
>
> CHAPTER 5
> Experiencing the Job Search: *making choices* 39

Part Two: Forming a Work that Endures: *weaving the story of Life/Work Direction* 45

> CHAPTER 6
> Many Mansions: *finding a starting point to weave* 47
>
> CHAPTER 7
> Laying a Foundation for a Life Work: *identifying warp threads* 59
>
> Chapter 8
> Creating Community: *seeing a pattern emerge* 75
>
> Chapter 9
> Looking in the Mirror: *examining the design* 87

Table of Contents

Part Three: Establishing a Direction: *interweaving others' callings*   95

   Chapter 10
   Bringing Life/Work Home: *envisioning a larger tapestry*   97

   Chapter 11
   On the Threshold: *adding colorful new threads*   105

   Chapter 12
   Becoming One in the Spirit: *blending colors into a new pattern*   119

   Chapter 13
   The Tapestry: *creation of the master weaver*   137

Epilogue   145

End Notes   147

Bibliographic Resources   151

Acknowledgments   155

TIMELINE

Don and Eunice Schatz arrive	1979	Scott Walker arrives in Boston
Many Mansions— Dick Faxon	1980	

1981 — Life/Work Direction incorporated

Change from group work to work with individuals.	1986	Scott Walker, Stephanie Smith and Carmel Cuyler participate in LWD
	1987	Scott and Louise Walker marry

1990 — Move LWD to Jamaica Plain to share Walker home

Dick Faxon retires; Carmel Cuyler joins part-time staff	1993	Walkers begin ministry at Cornerstone
	1996	Walkers' sabbatical– Threshold conceived
	1998	Threshold begins
	2004	Walkers' sabbatical

2005 — The strands of Life/Work Direction and Threshold merge

Eunice begins two-year Shalem Program in Spiritual Guidance	2007	Life/Work Direction under Walkers' leadership
Don Schatz retires	2010	

Introduction

*My frame was not hidden from You,
when I was being made in secret,
intricately woven in the depths of the earth.*
Psalm 139:15

WE ALL HAVE A STORY
I am writing this book for anyone who has asked, "What should I do with my life?" My instinctive response will always be, "Tell me your story." You change when you tell your story to another. You begin to see new meaning, to recognize how intricately woven are the threads of your life, and you begin to envision a way forward. I begin here by telling my own story—uncovering the way I moved into my calling.

I am writing especially for those of you who have walked through the doors of Life/Work Direction—either into the rugged storefront in Dorchester in the 1980s, or into the home environment in Jamaica Plain where we eventually landed. You understand the power of your own story as you shared it with us.

A simple idea motivates us to ask for story. We know that your calling in life is "where your deep gladness and the world's deep hunger meet."[1] Most people need reminders to identify their deep gladness. That is where story-telling helps. The world's deep hungers are everywhere. It is making the connection that is tricky.

WE ARE TELLING LIFE/WORK DIRECTION'S STORY
What is true for individuals is also true for Life/Work Direction as an organization. I am writing for those of you who have a fascination with the process of creating a work—in this case, an organism that can last through the decades. You know what it is like to envision something, take innocent first steps, contain the risks and hopes, and feel exhilaration in

the face of unfolding possibility. By telling our story, I invite you into the hidden workshop behind Life/Work Direction's visible exterior; the place where all the tools are kept, where the broken pieces and false steps are displayed, and the joyful memories of the process of creating are arrayed like photographs on the wall.

It is a good time to tell Life/Work Direction's story—about our birth, about the people who bore us into life and midwifed the delivery, about how we grew and the "village" of participants that helped shape our work. As we enter our fourth decade, a new generation is being served, and new leaders have joined us.

THE WEAVING OF A LIFE WORK

As I began writing the story, I became aware that I was observing the weaving of a tapestry. It seemed to be an apt metaphor to describe the varied strands of influence that converged in the shaping of Life/Work Direction. Weaving speaks in a language of pattern and symbol.

The vertical warp threads set the basic structure—those unalterable values on which the work is premised and which help to make it unique. For us, in creating the tapestry called Life/Work Direction, the warp threads stand out: our unwavering conviction that an integration between life and work—who you are and what you do—is essential, creating harmony between your inner and outer life.

The horizontal weft threads are an assortment of colors and textures, giving flexibility in choosing the program elements, varying the texture of the experience in the vocational process, and in adding vivid colors in the unique character of the staff.

Providentially, the intersection of warp and weft threads forms a cross whenever the two meet, creating a place of healing and redemption, and new life. The story in this book chronicles these crossings as a way of uncovering the larger pattern in our lives and in the organization we helped create.

I was at the loom in the 1980s, together with my husband Don Schatz and with our friend and Episcopal priest Dick Faxon, identifying the key warp threads, choosing the colors and working the shuttles. Even in those first years some additional colorful weft threads were appearing: Scott Walker was on the periphery at first, but he and his wife, Louise, added their vision and energy in various ways until it was time to begin weaving our callings together in the summer of 2005. A work of art emerged, the product of our joint undertaking.

The interlacing might seem serendipitous, almost random, if it were not for our conviction that an unseen Master Weaver was at work in us.

We only see dimly, working the tapestry from the underside. God is the Divine Weaver overseeing the creation of the pattern. The story I tell here flows from my appreciation of the process of the weaving itself. It has been the love of my life to be part of it—the weaving and the writing.

Prologue

THE DOOR CHIME SIGNALS THE START OF OUR DAY. We welcome you at the door, beckon you inside, and offer a cup of tea, before inviting you around the corner and into one of three chairs arranged around the table. Soft lamplight glows from three corners of the room as we settle into place.

A quiet moment, a few pleasantries exchanged, as we sit waiting. Then one of us speaks: "Tell us your story."

We listen. We take it in. We laugh and cry with you. We are delighted. We are surprised. We are hopeful. We begin to care. We don't know all its meanings, but we cherish the story, and you. We are called to walk with you in tracing the trajectory of your life, exploring your gifts in work, and discovering the direction of both.

Over the years, we watch to see what happens:

- As you discover the truth of who you are—by tracing the intricately woven threads of the tapestry of your life—an underlying pattern comes to light, the mark of the Creator who loves you unconditionally and whose image you bear.
- As you uncover your God-graced gifts—those traits that are a unique expression of how you were "formed in the womb" of God—you identify the marks of your deep gladness that point you to work that will fill you full.
- As you find a direction for your joy to overflow to others in life and work, you exude God's love to others.

A prayer arises:

> *You who are my Maker,*
> *you knew my name at the beginning*
> *and long to draw me into becoming who I fully am.*
> *Weave in and around our dreams and memories with your mercy's yarn*
> *to create our unique patterns beloved by you.*[2]

We whisper *Amen.*

PART ONE

Letting Life Reveal a Calling

seeing the pattern in the strands of life story

> "For we are what he has made us,
> created in Christ Jesus for good works,
> which God prepared beforehand
> to be our way of life."
> Ephesians 2:10

CHAPTER I

In the Beginning:
two colors appear

IF I WERE TO MARK A BEGINNING OF OUR LIFE and work and its direction in Boston, I would place it in a particular spot on the Mass Pike on the chilly March day in 1979 when we moved from Chicago to Boston. Don was piloting the U-Haul truck behind me as I navigated our way in a Plymouth Valiant, laden with our plants and other items too delicate to entrust to the truck. A soft rain was falling as we exited the last tollbooth in Cambridge and made our way down the expressway toward our eventual destination in Dorchester.

Out of the corner of my eye I spied a car speeding down an entry ramp and gauged my own speed accordingly, confident that the car entering would be yielding to the main traffic on the turnpike. Wrong. It zoomed onto the highway ahead of us with brazen foolhardiness. It was my first introduction to the fabled "Boston driver" and to the intricacies of maneuvering in a town (yes, town—Chicago was a city) where streets wind unpredictably following ancient cow paths and where different traffic habits apply.

Boston was going to be a place requiring an extra measure of alertness, where greater care must be taken to interweave others' actions with one's own. I would learn to tap the brake or accelerator pedals tentatively, as I approached those frequent entrance ramps along major arteries like Route 128, in order to keep traffic flowing smoothly. It would be a precise calibration, sensitizing me to the subtle (and not so subtle) impulses of others.

We learned to live the Boston way, after the more predictable geometry of Chicago streets and the infinitely harsher application of driving laws by Chicago policemen. Here in Boston, a cop might wave us on if we were making an improper turn. We decided that Boston driving habits were more relationally attuned and often efficient, especially when one needed to make an unexpected turn from the wrong lane — not a bad bargain.

❦

Why do I choose this moment to mark the beginning of a new life and work? It is the sense that one never creates from a completely blank slate. A beginning date is arbitrary, only necessary for statistical purposes. No, it was the incorporation of what was already here that made Life/Work Direction what it became. We had to yield to the flow, the energy, the pace already planted here by others. Yes, we would be bringing our own vibrant life force with us, the fruit of ten years spent in birthing the Urban Life Center in Chicago — a project that had engaged us since the early days of our marriage. It was a program for college students, providing an immersion in city life with a community of peers, including the bonus of earning a semester of college credit.

All the ferment and fervor of those ten years of solid achievement were left behind the day we wheeled out of the snowy driveway of our South Shore apartment and headed toward the East Coast.

Our encounter with Boston driving habits on that rainy day in March was symbolic of more than our entrance into a new culture. It also signaled an ending for us. The Urban Life Center was past; what would comprise the center of our life in this new urban environment? We did not yet know on that March day in 1979. It would require time to bring it to life, for we did not yet discern the direction of that work.

❦

Another energy was at work as we raced down that expressway heading toward Dorchester. A hundred miles away in the Berkshires, a senior at Williams College, Scott Walker, was contemplating his own return to Dorchester in June. He was remembering his own immersion in urban living the previous summer as a college intern there. He was strongly affected by the experience, just as our Urban Life Center students in Chicago were. Scott had thrived in the program and he would be returning to Dorchester to co-direct it just three months after our arrival.

At the time none of us knew how our paths were destined to cross at significant intervals during the next three decades, nor did we anticipate the way those crossings would affect our life work and its direction.

In Scott's words

Sitting in my dorm room in the winter of 1979, I flipped the button on a tiny tape recorder on my desk. A cacophony of street sounds blasted into the silence of the room, followed by voices of children at play, then the buzz of traffic—the sizzle of the wheels of a bus on a rainy pavement, the screech of a fire siren splitting the air, then a burst of gospel music from a church choir, followed by the mellow baritone of Stevie Wonder. I had made this tape the previous summer in order to hold on to the sense of a place that was so strikingly different from the worlds I knew. I taped the sounds as I rode the subway and captured the siren choruses in the night outside the window of our makeshift dorm on the upper floors of Mount Calvary Holiness Church off Blue Hill Avenue, a former synagogue and Hebrew school. To me, these were vibrant sounds of life.

I had a romanticized view of the city when I arrived. It was as if I were a visitor to a foreign country. I took pictures of open fire hydrants, reveling in the sight of urban streams rippling down asphalt streets.

My view of the city was punctuated by the experience of getting mugged that summer, and in a rather frightening way. I fled to the little house church I was serving in my internship to seek refuge and support. I was angry, but I did not run away to the serenity of my hometown in Connecticut, much to the surprise of the pastor and his wife. I remember the white cop who filed the police report that night. His parting words caught me off guard. "Don't hold this against these people. There are plenty of good folks in this neighborhood." In the tense racial climate of Boston at the time, his concern surprised me. Inner city reality was both harder and softer than I knew.

I was contemplating my return to Dorchester in the summer of 1979 to be part of the same internship program, this time as co-director. I don't remember much about my senior year. It became a long corridor leading me back to Boston.

The day before graduation, I made one last push to finish a late paper. When I walked with my class the next day I remember being worn out and more conscious of what lay ahead of me than of the four years I was leaving behind. Unlike most of my peers who traveled home with their parents that afternoon, I stayed in Williamstown that night so that I could catch the early bus to Boston. I was eager to get started on my first job.

We were three persons entering the city at the same time, but at different life stages. Scott was at the beginning of finding his life work, even as Don and I were at the midpoint in our lives and going through a metamorphosis. Yet we shared a common impulse. Scott was looking for a way to live out his faith among the poor and marginalized. Don and I had been shepherding Christian college students through a similar experience. The Urban Life Center sprang from the soil of the turbulent sixties and seventies in an environment ripe for experimentation. Students in Christian colleges were itching to move away from their isolated rural and suburban campuses and into the vortex of Carl Sandburg's "city of big shoulders" hunched on the shores of Lake Michigan. In Chicago, tribal ethnicities and race clashed, the wealthy and the poor were sharply segregated, and great art and architecture rubbed up against the urban blight of industry and slums. We came to Boston fresh from that experience, yet longing to find a deeper way of working—Don with his art, by writing poetry, and I with my desire to continue supporting people as they seek meaning and direction.

It would not take long before these three threads would interweave to form the story of Life/Work Direction that unfolds in these pages.

CHAPTER 2

Endings:
letting go of some strands

O UR BASIC QUESTION IN COMING TO BOSTON was classic: What should we do with our lives? The question was stark and real for us on the survival level. However, rushing ahead on a full-scale job search would not answer the question deeply, because both Don and I were in a major life transition.

In his book *Transitions,* William Bridges helpfully describes three necessary stages in this process: ending the old, beginning the new, and negotiating a frustrating and less understood "neutral zone" in between.[3] Endings, according to Bridges, involve a three-pronged process of disengagement, displacement, and disenchantment. He emphasizes the need to pay careful attention to endings in order to clarify the deeper reasons for leaving a situation, and to avoid making false or inappropriate starts on new endeavors.

DISENGAGEMENT
I was not wise enough to see this transition pattern clearly at the time. We thought that terminating our apartment lease and handing our resignation letter to the board of the Urban Life Center; then packing all our belongings into a truck, wrapping every article of furniture in blankets as a shield against the jostle of the road, and placing our carefully tended plants in the back seat of the Plymouth sheathed in plastic to protect them from the chill as we traveled, were sufficient proof of our deliberate uprooting from the past.

Like so many others, Don and I also counted on our carefully planned geographic move to mark a firm ending to our life in Chicago. Just the process of driving east would work its magic—passing across the flat Midwestern terrain, over the gently rolling Allegheny Mountains, into the Berkshires, and finally arriving in the swell-and-swale topography of New England dotted with its signature Cape Cod houses nestled among pines and firs. We relished the preponderance of evergreens here, after the dominance of the deciduous elms and cottonwoods and oaks of the prairies.

We were charmed by the labyrinthine design of Boston streets, feeling only an occasional nostalgic twinge for Chicago's post-Great Fire street grid with its geometric precision. We never got lost in Chicago; numbers on every street pole marked our exact latitude and longitude. In Boston, streets might twist and turn and retain the same name, whereas going straight ahead often landed me on another street.

These external changes were deceptive, diverting our attention from the necessary internal changes. We were heading into the often-neglected neutral zone of which Bridges speaks, a place that feels like nowhere—being lost and at sea.

THE DEEPER LEVEL OF DISPLACEMENT

These outer signs of disengagement masked an unspoken undercurrent of feeling. This move was not just about leaving our apartment and our work; something more basic was happening—displacement.

This was harshest for me. I had surrendered my role as one of the founders and a co-director of the Urban Life Center, a role with which I was strongly identified from its inception. I was unknown in Boston, a mixed blessing. On one hand, I would have to make my own way, a daunting task. On the other hand, it was an opportunity to change—there were some aspects of my performance and approach that I regretted. I had sometimes been indirect in my leadership at the Center, working with other strong independent personalities. I had envisioned creative collaboration in shaping things, but became wobbly when asking others to move in a new direction. Could something new emerge in me on the Atlantic coast, a deeper current in my life and work?

A second loss for me was moving away from the richness of thirty-five years of personal associations—my community. It was not just my colleagues at the Urban Life Center. I had lived in the Chicago area since I was eight years old, and a web of supporting and encouraging friendships had grown around me, people who looked to me for stimulus and caring, and from whom I expected the same.

As I write this today, thirty years later, I see the enormity of these losses. I was less aware at the time, so eager was I both to leave Chicago and to head into a new life in the East. We had considered it thoughtfully, and made careful preparations; there was not much looking back.

Don's experience took a more complex tilt. The future beckoned to him, offering an inviting new identity that excited him. Instead of mourning a loss, he faced the unknown with expectancy, more eager than I to leave the past. It was his first major move, having lived all his life in Chicago as the eldest son of a close-knit Jewish extended family. They referred to him as "Donny"—a moniker of which he had tired. His extended family and friends had seen him as a slightly eccentric artist and loner and had left him to fend for himself. For him to attend to his own artistic development required a new environment where he could enter the world in his own right.

His voice as a poet carried the echoes of the Holocaust—a group voice. He longed to find his individual voice. By marrying me, and stepping into the Christian community, a larger world opened to him and his personal voice was born. Perhaps Boston was a place where he could develop as a poet and writer.

ENDINGS TAKE TIME
If I just focus on that thousand-mile move, I will obscure the complexity of endings, how they take place over a considerable period of time. Our resignation in 1979 was not precipitous. Vague dissatisfactions had begun to detach us from our life and work in Chicago at the Center at least two years earlier, when we had hired a younger person, Scott Chesebro, a Sociology teacher from Tabor College in Kansas, to join the Urban Life Center staff. We did not know then that we were grooming him to assume the director role, and he may not have seen it that way himself. Today, thirty-two years later, Scott is still at the helm of the Urban Life Center (now called Chicago Center for Urban Life and Culture), and deserves much of the credit for shaping it into a lively force. When he and his wife arrived in 1977, such aspirations were not explicitly voiced. We could pretend to ourselves and others that the Center was simply expanding and Don and I were staying on.

Unwittingly, I had begun preparing myself for our move by a gradual shift in my interests within my role at the Urban Life Center. I liked shaping the curriculum with others. I was good at administrative detail, setting up systems and organizing files, and Don and I enjoyed traveling to college campuses each semester to recruit students. But increasingly we found our work with the board difficult and cumbersome—a little like herding cats. I did my part poorly. Meanwhile, my day-to-day contact with students had whetted my appetite for more person-to-person work.

Now I understand why I responded so strongly to a picture that one student drew for me before I left and that now hangs in my hallway at Life/Work Direction. It depicts simply two chairs facing each other in front of the ivy-covered windowpanes. It was where I so often sat with students, fully engaged as they plied me with the perennial question— "what should I do with my life?" They were asking questions about vocation.

And in fact, so was I.

HINTS OF A NEW VOCATION APPEAR

The undercurrent of restlessness in my role as director coincided with the emergence of interest in vocational questions in the academic culture at the time. When Richard Bolles' nationally popular book *What Color is Your Parachute*[4] appeared, I pounced on it. I began looking for the people in Chicago who were exploring these issues.

I did not have to wait long. The American Association for Higher Education was meeting in Chicago that spring, and by virtue of my position at the Urban Life Center, I attended. Students in colleges everywhere were dissatisfied with the way college prepared them for work after graduation. This became the impetus behind a groundswell of enthusiasm for experiential programs like the Urban Life Center among faculty and administrators in higher education.

The conference program listed a session on "Identifying Transferable Skills." It took place in an obscure basement location, where the leader was basing his presentation on Richard Bolles' book. I was fascinated. Not only was the material applicable to my own searching for change in my career; I had instinctively used similar methods in helping Urban Life Center students obtain internships. I had a natural aptitude for career counseling.

I began networking in the Chicago area, and discovered some practitioners who used the term "Life Work Planning." Those words resonated with me. I was at home with the wholistic approach of blending concerns of life with work. I decided to offer a few workshops and individual sessions for friends as an experiment. I designed a crude flyer, made up a title for my embryonic venture using my initials (CareERS – "Put the Care in Care-ers"), and began offering workshops on the side while still retaining my role at the Urban Life Center.

One aspect of my experiment turned out to be predictive of the style that would later mark our approach at Life/Work Direction. After a client, Bob, had a few individual sessions with me, he asked if he could draw in a few other friends for our next session in order to get feedback from a diverse group. I corralled my husband, and Bob asked Bruce and Ruth, two wise friends who knew all of us, to join in. The following week, five of us sat in our living room as Bob described dilemmas he was facing in changing the trajectory of his life and work. We were to listen carefully, then ask pertinent and probing questions to help him think through the decisions he was making.

At the end of the evening, Bruce remarked wistfully, "This was great. Can I take a turn? Could we meet again?" We met four more times, so that each member of the group could take center stage for an evening, with the rest of us attentively responding. I felt a palpable creative energy in the room as we shared our diverse perspectives with the person on stage. It meant that henceforth I would be less satisfied with the one-on-one counseling model, where the subtle implication of authority resting with the counselor supplants the cooperative spirit that generates diversity of outcomes. Life/Work Direction would extend that idea by always having two or three staff persons working together with the same participant on life/work questions. It would be an important point, and distinctive of an approach we would find useful later.

My excitement about vocation was shifting to this new possibility of life work planning, giving me the handle I needed for approaching the move to a new city. I had the requisite "transferable skills," paving the way for crafting a résumé that would demonstrate my readiness for this kind of work.

Don was monitoring my shift in perspective closely. He saw my growing attraction to individual work with students using my strong psychological orientation. He was all set to leave both the Urban Life Center and Chicago. He was waiting for me to be ready. He counted on me finding something I wanted to do wherever we landed.

Although I had only the foggiest notion of how I would be received in my new environment in Boston, I proceeded with cheerful optimism. The field of life/work planning was too new to have established formal credentials. If this were the field I wanted to enter, having to find work on my own in a new city was perfect preparation. I had irrepressible hope because I was engaged in finding my own vocation. I now know this to be a cardinal principle in vocational choice: we are often drawn toward helping others with something we are in the process of learning ourselves.

Surely there would be some place in Boston that would welcome us with open arms, I thought idealistically. The environment into which we were heading would make the extent of our transition clear, in fact searingly so, because we were not prepared for the disenchantment that can follow disengagement and displacement.

CHAPTER 3

The End of Ideals:
when the colors fade

1979

THE CHOICE OF BOSTON WAS SOMEWHAT ARBITRARY, but in the end, providential. A friend offered us an apartment in a building in Dorchester for $110 a month—a mind-bogglingly low rent. Since we were strapped for cash by the cost of the move, we considered this a God-sent affirmation of our choice.

We considered Washington, D. C., but decided the federal government's imposing presence dwarfed the city and its inhabitants. Boston became an ideal place to land with its long history and rich culture, including some sixty institutions of higher education. We were used to the stimulus student life provided. And, as Don pointed out, "It's closer to Europe!" His own wanderings in Europe had proved a seminal impetus for his art, resulting in his transition from painting to writing poetry. The use of words became his expressive art. His poetry linked him to Europe and to his Jewish ancestry, and to the darkness of Holocaust that lingers over much of his writing.

Don's sense of himself in his early childhood was as a secular Jew. But in 1945, at the age of eight, everything changed; that identity no longer felt safe. He told me:

My uncle, Norman Schatz, had returned from World War II, where he had taken part in the liberation of Jewish victims at Buchenwald concentra-

tion camp. He was a messenger for our family. We saw horrifying photos of heaped up corpses being shoveled into mass graves. The images burned themselves onto my brain. It could have been me, I suddenly realized, as I listened to family members murmuring in the background and heard my mother crying. From that point on, my life was shadowed by the metaphor of the Holocaust.

During high school years, Don poured out his angst playing jazz on his trumpet. Then he turned to art, a way of working out his feelings on an unconscious level. He covered huge canvases with haunting paintings of hollow-eyed figures reminiscent of the concentration camp victims. "But the paintings were not tied to history," he said. "In Boston I got in touch with history."

Coming to Boston, Don quickly picked up the pace of life here, the language, the way people talked, as he walked around Harvard Square. The sense of his calling as an artist could find an independent root here, apart from his early life. He quickly intuited that here in New England he might find a literary and artistic sensibility that would nurture his poetic work and provide a new grounding, one more native to his character.

※

I had my own familial threads tying me to New England. I was born in New Hampshire and only moved to the Midwest at the age of seven. My parents had met in Boston while attending Gordon College of Theology and Mission (as it was then called) on the Fenway. Their honeymoon apartment was in Roxbury, a scant half mile from where we now live in Jamaica Plain.

My father's past was much on my mind, for he had died six months before we moved. I had read his journals and felt acquainted with his life in Cambridge during his years at Harvard, first as an undergraduate, then in law school. I would be walking under the same elms that shaded him as he walked across Harvard Yard. I would be taking advantage of the same "T" that took him, in 1910, in trolley cars throughout all of eastern Massachusetts—as far as Cape Cod to the east, and Waverly to the west, where he often walked to Walden Pond from the end of the line.

His side of my family provided me with another tie. We learned that our Dorchester apartment was located near "Upham's Corner," a name that rang a bell for me, since I was named for my great grandmother Mary Eunice Upham. Many of my ancestors are buried in the cemetery plot in Upham's Corner. I would later discover other ancestors who had participated in historic events in Boston—on my father's side, Jason Russell who was gunned down by the British in April of 1775, and whose memory is preserved in a museum in Arlington; and on my mother's side, Mary Dyer, a Quaker who was hanged on the Boston Common in 1660 for her defiance of the authorities in holding to her religious beliefs, and whose statue stands in front of the State House to this day as a reminder of past harshness in today's reputedly "liberal" commonwealth.

Boston ought to be home for me, but I was not so sure that day in March as we made the final turn and pulled up in front of our apartment at 23 Maryland Street. Don maneuvered the bulky U-Haul truck down the narrow one-way street, crowded with parked cars on both sides. Instead of the solid brick buildings several stories high to which he was accustomed all his life in Chicago, he eyed warily the row of closely set wooden triple-deckers immediately bordering the sidewalk, a signature of Boston's architectural style. Several vacant lots yawned menacingly across the street, an ominous sign of burned out buildings. We had dropped into another world.

Our first human encounter with that world came when Jimmy, a small spry man, jumped off the front steps of our apartment building and greeted us cheerfully. He offered to help us unpack. Naively, we struck up a conversation, unaware that he was casing our load for any choice items that might one day be removed. I began to be a little suspicious when he volunteered suggestions for a way to siphon gas out of somebody else's tank. He appeared to have a number of such skills on his résumé. We would soon learn their full range. In a few weeks, he found a way to secretly tap into our phone line to make long distance calls, managed to siphon off oil from our furnace during the harsh winter, and eventually—when the landlord terminated his lease a year later—he tried to burn the house down. He wound up in prison, charged with one hundred counts of arson. Now we grasped the significance of those vacant burned out lots across the street. For Don, these events accentuated his sense of being a Jewish Displaced Person. "We could be burned alive by the arsonist upstairs," he said.

We were soon to learn how green we were. We had lived in a predominantly middle class black community on Chicago's South Shore, and had experienced the usual urban difficulties common in the 1970s. Like all my buddies at the University of Chicago, we had been ripped off—as the saying went—more than ten times in our first decade of marriage. It was a stubborn badge of honor marking our insistence on not being part of white flight to the suburbs. We treated our losses casually since a number of these occasions involved persons we knew: thirteen-year-old Frankie, who lived upstairs, and who left his big sneaker footprints on our linoleum floor, leading to the place where a camera he admired had once hung on a hook; and José, a musician, who came over to jam one night, and left with a twenty dollar bill I had carelessly left in an open purse on a table.

Theft did not appear to be the prime problem on Maryland Street. Rather it appeared to be a place for street clashes. A policeman once told us, "Maryland Street? When I was a kid we used to come to Maryland Street to fight." *Great,* we thought. The street was occupied by poor white families with the predictable array of problems: alcoholism, various forms of abuse, and grinding poverty. But I noticed that no one locked his front door.

A Cambodian family moved in across the street, and we made friendly gestures toward them. Race had been an issue in our Chicago experience, and we were well attuned to it. Here our welcoming gestures were a sign to our neighbors that we were on the wrong side of the issue. Some neighbors shouted epithets at us, splashed egg on our window, and slashed the tires on our car. The message was clear: don't make the Cambodians feel welcome on this turf.

We did not know how to live according to our lofty ideals in this community. Race clashed with class, and we were caught in the middle. Most of the neighbors were white like us, but there were subtle signs of our educated background and attitudes that marked us as a different class. We felt alone and outside.

I was acutely aware of the absence of the bourgeois trappings I'd grown used to in my South Side Chicago community. The houses on Maryland Street weren't carpeted. The sinks stood alone in the kitchens, bereft of cabinets. The refrigerators didn't defrost themselves. The pipes weren't all behind walls; some were in plain view. Our basement had a dirt floor. The dogs weren't on leash (and consequently didn't need to bark so much to proclaim their territory). Kids played in the streets constantly, and mothers screamed at them. Classical music, jazz, great art, discussion of ideas, going to the museum—these were for folks across the river in Cambridge, not Dorchester.

I was dismayed at my own reactions. I was alternately critical of and horrified by my surroundings. To attempt to identify with my neighbors seemed to be totally out of the question. It appeared that "downward mobility" didn't suit me well, despite my radical rhetoric.

My disorientation came to a climax one Sunday morning when Don and I ventured out to Boston's South End to worship at church. The experience was electrifying in itself, and was compounded by all the raw emotions surrounding our uprooted state. But at such times there is also more clarity.

Stepping inside, we instantly felt the neighborliness, as a friendly tail-wagging dog bounded through the foyer, sniffing at people as they entered. A lady in the third row had a small cache of biscuits that she surreptitiously distributed to the stray dog as members assembled.

I kept looking for some distinguishing mark of commonality. Was this a church of poor people? Of Latinos? Of street folks? There seemed to be one of every category I could identify. The organist paused between chords of her prelude to sign to two obviously deaf persons in the front row. Later, she interpreted the entire sermon for them. A second dog made his appearance shortly, this one leading his mistress, who was blind. She sat in her chair, rocking back and forth.

I was struck by the variety of skin colors. Every two or three chairs, the colors changed. But still no categories stuck. Some were well dressed, some shabby. Some faces looked gaunt and worried, a little out-of-touch. Others appeared fresh from college studies, alert and carefree.

When we bowed to pray, the weight of the crushing burdens of this tiny congregation momentarily overwhelmed me. Physical and mental disability, poverty, injustice, oppression, discrimination all crowded together in my consciousness. I was painfully aware of my clear-eyed gaze and relatively unworn face, so free of cares.

I was torn. On the one hand, I wanted to come and live in the midst of these people. I wanted to share their love and gifts. It was obvious to me that they had these to give. Yet I wanted to run away. I didn't want to know they existed at all. I wanted to be with people who looked like me, talked and thought like me.

Familiarity and security? Or risk and challenge? I was surprised—and distressed—to find I was comfortable with neither. We came to Boston full of pride for our progressive attitudes toward urban problems, our spirit of helpfulness to those in need. We sincerely believed that this was in alignment with the way Jesus taught, but we were proving failures in living out those beliefs on a practical level in daily life. Our capacity to live out ideals came crashing down, and we felt defeated and broken in spirit. Now we were the ones needing help and rest.

*

We also needed jobs—fast! Don's adjustment was far smoother than mine. He landed a job selling art prints at the Harvard Coop. He warmed to the intellectual energy buzzing around the famous bookstore. Sometimes while scanning a credit card for a customer, he would blink, seeing the name of a Nobel Prize winner. The Harvard atmosphere provided a fertile place for memories of the Transcendentalists, followed by a trail of influential thinkers streaming from within those ivied walls. Don said, "I was reborn here. I saw the archetypal dimension of my life." He was in a familiar world—a confluence of students and academics tied together by their attachment to the arts, to science, to literature, to philosophy, rather than to place. They too were exiles, in a way, and fellow travelers in time and space. As an artist and poet, he was accustomed to earning money at something other than his true vocation. A cultured environment was stimulus enough.

I gravitated toward temporary typing jobs—the fastest way for me to generate income. I experienced instant role displacement. I'd been used to the freedom and prestige of a director role. Now I was being treated like a secretary, told to move as though from one chalk mark to another on a pre-arranged stage. The put-downs were subtle and unintended, but they were there—like the assumption that I was incapable of anything beyond blind copy work and counting spaces from the left-hand margin. My feminist awareness sprang to life after a period of dormancy, as I lived in the shadow of a liberal university and shouldered major work responsibilities.

On my way home from work, sitting in the subway with my unknown neighbors, I began to identify with them: people who go to work every day, are told what to do, receive very little pay, and live from one pay check to the next. Meanwhile, Don and I were edging slowly but surely toward the brink of insolvency. The move to Boston, the unexpected trips West for two family funerals, and fifteen hundred dollars worth of repairs on our aging Plymouth Valiant, plus a hungry, oil-guzzling (and occasionally "leaking") furnace—all these took their toll on our modest resources.

I got scared. I sat down with Don to reconnoiter. Why were we here? What was the meaning of this consummate concern with survival? Here we were in Dorchester, afraid we'd run out of oil before we had the money to pay for it and that our cash on hand wouldn't last until pay day. I was beginning to identify with my neighbors more than I had intended. I began observing them closely. How did they manage the cost of oil? Were they also sitting around in their houses with sweaters and socks piled on?

My discoveries surprised me. In the first place, no one else in Boston seemed to be used to the overheated apartments to which I had become accustomed in Chicago. I learned to wear a few more layers, keep active, and send messages to my body to adjust to a lower temperature over-all. I began to see that humor, friendship, and family ties were strong and important outlets for people on the street: an ongoing card game at the corner store in a back room, men wearing hats and swapping stories with one another; a mother across the street, always on the front porch watching her children, carrying on conversations with other women leaning out of second-story windows; eleven-year-old Stanley, who offered to help me pick up trash and who knocked often, asking, "Anything you need at the store?"—his inventive way of earning pocket money.

I was still haunted by the tired faces of the women coming off the subway at the end of a working day. Their jobs did not confer dignity and meaning, causing a harsh but necessary separation between personal and work life. Even the menial jobs I took at first were more than some of my neighbors had. I had been busy preaching meaningful careers, but I had to live without that for a time, and was relieved to find I didn't fall apart without a professional work role.

It was a humbling experience and an insight I would prize. I could no longer look at people from the outside, according to sociological categories taught me during my Master's program at the University of Chicago. Immersion in this new environment was forcing me to examine my assumptions about who I was, and how I fit into the world. I had arrived in Boston with a full head of steam, energized by past accomplishments and eager to begin a new life work. Now I was among the unemployed, and facing a job search for the first time in my life. It was necessary preparation for someone who hoped to help others find meaningful work.

Living in Boston had forced us to come to terms with opposing energies—some stimulating and vital, adding freshness and vigor, and others difficult and taxing, stripping us down to the level of basic survival. As we entered this new chapter of life, a few blocks away in Dorchester, Scott Walker was beginning his post-college life in an apartment not far from where we lived. He too was adjusting to daily life in the city.

In Scott's words:

I was full of idealism. At Williams College, my faith was influenced by a campus Christian fellowship group that was concerned about social justice. I found thoughtful people who were reading the writings of Jim Wallis at Sojourners, William Stringfellow, and professors at the Institute for Christian Study in Toronto. The issues of social justice resonated with me, and I was struck by the idea of God dwelling among the poor and outcast.

In the spring of 1978, Roger Dewey, the founder of Christians for Urban

Justice (CUJ), visited Williams to recruit students to a new urban immersion and service experience in Boston during the coming summer. I signed up immediately, a logical next step as I was increasingly drawn towards a faith that identified with those "outside" and dispossessed.

The program fed directly into my desire for both intellectual and experiential engagement. A couple from Gordon Conwell Seminary launched the program that summer, overseeing ten college interns. They engaged us in theological reflection on our work in the city and had us read a rich repertoire of writings on Christian social justice. Best of all, we were encouraged to memorize Scripture passages on God's concern for the poor, an enrichment I will always prize. This left a deep impression and I still can recite many of them.

Experience in the summer internship program, as participant in 1978, and then as leader in 1979, whetted my appetite to put down roots here in Boston's inner city. I wanted to live out the gospel in the way Jesus exemplified it in his identification with the poor.

It helped that I came to Dorchester with my best friend, Stocky Wulsin, with whom I shared an interest in city ministry. Stocky and I used to get together at the close of each college year and talk about how the year had gone. He had taken part in a compelling ministry experience in Newark, New Jersey, the summer before. After our graduation, we decided to throw our lots in together to invest further in inner city service and learning. Stocky decided to join me in moving permanently to Boston at the end of the summer to look for housing together and then for work.

That September we landed on the top floor of Paul and Jan Bothwell's house. Paul was the pastor of a start-up house church, Jesus Helps Neighborhood Baptist, where I had served the previous summer. Paul had become a mentor to me. He was ten years older, a man who had grown up abroad with missionary parents but who now had a keen sense of calling to help start inner city churches. He welcomed us to get our bearings under his roof while we looked for our own apartment. In addition he offered to meet with us regularly for informal supervision and cross-cultural reflection as we became involved in building relationships and helping out within the church and neighborhood. I was grateful for his guidance, and I think he appreciated our fresh energy and enthusiasm regardless of how green we were.

A month later Stocky and I set up shop in our own apartment four blocks away from the church, right on the line between Dorchester and Roxbury. In our mostly black neighborhood, we soon got the nicknames Starsky and Hutch, after a television series popular at the time featuring a white law enforcement duo of the plainclothes type. No one knew what to make of us. It was apparent that we were on a mission of some sort. Though seen as a "foreigner," I began to feel at home, relishing the faith adventure in a new season.

CUJ provided another community of support, where I was preparing for the summer internship program. Roger was seen as a 60s radical in the Christian community in Boston, always starting innovative programs, such as a home weatherization drive. With others, I set up an energy-efficiency demonstration in a house owned by CUJ, and helped in a church-sponsored program that involved going into parishioner's homes with groups of volunteers to install weatherization materials that increased fuel efficiency and protected against the cold.

I also found a circle of likeminded peers in the small intentional community gathered around CUJ—recent college graduates who had come to Boston with a similar desire to live out the Gospel in the inner city. Most of them worked other jobs in and around Boston, like teaching or computer programming, and spent their free time investing in the work and worship life at CUJ. My role at CUJ was different. I worked there during the day as a staff member and spent most of my weekend and free time in my home and church community in a different part of Dorchester. Even so, I crossed paths enough with members of the CUJ community to develop good friendships. Ours was a common pilgrimage. Several of these friends would eventually find their way to Life/Work Direction—Stephanie Smith, Scott Heald, Joe and Mary Lou Verla.

Another support available to me was the Emmanuel Gospel Center in the South End led by Doug and Judy Hall. I respected the Center as being perhaps the sturdiest and longest lasting force in Boston for developing a vibrant multi-racial approach to recognizing the presence of Christ in the city. I met many of their staff through my friendship with the Bothwells, whose church-planting ministry was greatly aided by the resources of the Center. The Center's sense of mission was that of being dedicated servants of the churches of Boston, blending evangelistic zeal with scholarly, sociological reflection in a uniquely quirky way. While I appreciated their wisdom and example, I remember feeling a little self-conscious and uncomfortable around them. They were quick to question the value of short-term engagements in ministry and regularly trumpeted the possible counterproductivity of efforts to help the poor, especially by inexperienced altruistic outsiders who viewed themselves as gifted. Their sobriety was good for me.

I eventually moved on from the Jesus Helps Church and community, and settled in Upham's Corner to share a house with several peers. I began attending Dorchester Temple Baptist Church, pastored by Dan and Sharon Buttry. It was an important move for me. My first four years in the city had shown me how little I knew and how much my efforts to give were influenced by my own needs. It felt more honest moving to a church where I was not immediately cast in a leadership role. Dorchester Temple was a larger, more diverse congregation where the Buttrys had developed a multi-ethnic leadership team. In that setting I experienced the work of racial reconciliation and community building more as an indigenous endeavor between many people of different backgrounds rather than something chiefly led by educated white people. I went to church there first to receive rather than to minister to others, a healthy change.

That year, in 1983, I took the month of January to go on retreat back home in Connecticut. I was seeking God's guidance for next steps in my life. I now felt out of place in the role of urban missionary, as I had known it. I still felt compelled to be in the city and live out the gospel in concern for the poor, but doing this in the context of a church or Christian service organization no longer felt like the right fit for me. During my retreat at home I read through the Gospel of Luke and kept a journal of my reflections. After a few weeks I clearly sensed God inviting me, "Give Me what you love," which I immediately recognized to be my steady gravitational pull toward education—creating curriculum, leading discussion groups, teaching—all the activities I had loved most about the CUJ summer internship program. There was a calling here that fit the shape of my heart. I decided to test the waters of high school teaching by starting to substitute teach in the Boston Public Schools.

Somewhere around this time, I decided to seek out a counselor at the Danielsen Center at Boston University. It was here that I began to see that identification with the poor began with me—as I came to recognize my poverty of spirit.

Poverty of spirit was where Don and I were beginning too. It is where we all begin, not yet seeing the pattern God is weaving in our life tapestries.

CHAPTER 4

How a Calling is Shaped:
tracing the origins of the design

WHEN I LOOK BACK OVER MY LIFETIME, I see the underlying meaning in the psalmist's declaration that "God formed me"—starting in the womb. My orientation to the world of work began in childhood. Now that I have spent three decades in assisting other people to find their life work and its direction, I know the importance of that major first step in the vocational process—telling our life story. Our history is full of clues as to what has given us energy all our lives. I have told my life story elsewhere—the memoir called *Still Woman Moving*[5]—but my work history is salient here. I need to tease out the origin of my dreams of fulfillment and my characteristic attitudes and approaches to simple tasks and requirements.

Writing this today, I am astonished that I have paid so little attention to these in my own case. But it all comes flooding back to me now, giving me flashes of insight. In 1979, my attention was focused on the job search. The need for survival loomed large. Now, I can step back and begin to see the pattern in my work experience and how every choice I made was critical to the person I became by the time I arrived in Boston.

BEING SHAPED BY EARLY WORK EXPERIENCE
As a young person, I took work for granted. My childhood took place in the rural New England of the 1930s where physical labor was required for the basic necessities of daily living. If I wanted a drink of cold water, I

had to push the handle of the pump in the cast iron kitchen sink. Cooking cereal began at dawn with Mother stoking the fire in the wood stove. Corn, string beans, and tomatoes came from a garden out back that had to be hoed regularly. Washday meant pressing my knuckles against a scrub board. Ironing clothes required me to lift a heavy flatiron from the back of the stove, then maneuver it cautiously across a shirt on a rickety ironing board, being careful not to scorch the fabric.

An early entrepreneurial streak cropped up at the age of six. I set up a lemonade stand in front of our New Hampshire home on Highway 202. Passersby pulled over on a hot summer day and dropped two pennies into my box in return for a glass of fresh-squeezed lemonade. No store concentrate for me.

A more sophisticated version of entrepreneurship emerged in a cooperative venture in sixth grade with two friends in a midwestern college town where we had moved. The three of us came into possession of a box of tongue depressors and decided this was not a resource to be wasted, but raw material awaiting our primitive creative touch. Using alphabet soup letters glued onto the surface we spelled out simple slogans—"God Answers Prayer" and "Jesus Never Fails," turning each depressor into a plaque that we brazenly hawked to college students for fifteen cents. Our success prompted us to switch to a more elaborate medium, using Plaster of Paris molds, for which we charged a quarter. After a few weeks, we split the profits, and I bought a pair of roller skates with my share.

Only once do I remember applying for a job. I was sixteen, and entitled to enter the work force. I needed extra cash at Christmas and wanted to work during vacation like my fellow students. A sign in the window of the attractive-sounding "Sweet Shop," located conveniently next door to the theatre, advertised an opening. As I recall, my father went in with me to apply. The rest was up to me. For ten days, I stood (sitting not allowed) before a long counter in the room behind the store facing what seemed like acres of chocolates waiting to be packed into one-pound boxes during the Christmas season. The proprietor and her husband hunched over a stove in the back stirring huge vats of chocolate, talking volubly with each other, but never including me in their conversation.

I stared at my workspace. All those chocolates! And hand-dipped at that! How would I resist this tempting array? As it turned out, temptation ceased shortly after I began my job, which was boring beyond belief, and any excitement about eating chocolates paled by the time I had spent a couple of eight-hour days packing them. It was my first and only experience in what amounted to a sweatshop, the sole member of a nonexistent assembly line. The money wasn't worth enduring the boredom. I vowed never to punch a clock again.

The combination of my early life at home and my participation in these fledgling enterprises created strong connections in my mind between physical effort and productivity. This made it natural for me to gravitate to the mundane tasks involved in a string of part-time jobs that helped me earn my way through college: washing dishes, mopping floors, cleaning cupboards. I didn't think of these student experiences as real jobs. Working part-time was just something most of us did, and these simple jobs were easy to obtain in a college town.

One such job was a pleasurable short-term stint as chambermaid at the college dorm prior to the opening of the fall semester. My friend Nancy and I thought it would be more fun and efficient to team up together in using the militarily precise bed-changing methods we had learned in Home Nursing class the previous spring. We treated the task as musical choreography, developing a smooth rhythm of coordinated movements, each of us on one side of the bed: fluff out the sheet, secure it at the top, smooth it down to the foot of the bed, deftly miter the corners according to army regulations. It might be considered demeaning work, but we elevated it to an art and relished the harmony of the flow. We had prior experience in this kind of coordination: painting a picket fence together when we were thirteen, each perched on a side, slapping paint on the pickets with sufficient force to cover both pickets and ourselves. In both situations, the rhythm of the work served as background for animated conversation between us.

It was the job as "morning toast girl" in the dining hall on my Wheaton College campus during my junior year that drew out my best efforts. In those benighted days of class differentiation, there were two dining halls on campus—the "upper" on the first floor and in the basement below it, the "lower" dining hall that served the more indigent students. I felt uneasy with the distinction. I ate in "upper," but the circumstances of my life as a Depression baby in the home of a poorly paid minister who was periodically unemployed made me feel a certain kinship with those students who ate below. I noted there was less variety in the portions served, making "seconds"—consisting of a slice of bread drenched in gravy—an important staple in "lower." The students good-humoredly called it Wheaton Steak without a hint of condescension. So I ate above, as most students did, and worked below.

I arrived at work the first day at 6 a.m., my hair protectively sheathed in a net, and surveyed my surroundings. Rudy, the cook, was close by to supervise since the kitchen for both dining halls was in the basement adjacent to "lower." He made me a little nervous, jokingly referring to the pet rat that occasionally came scurrying out of a hole. He pointed to the heating pipes standing just above the cutting boards and workspace. "That's where he plays at night," Rudy told me.

I soon learned the trick to my job. There was no modern equipment for toasting. Instead I had to array a dozen slices of bread (the Wonder Bread variety was in style) on a rack, shove it into the huge old-fashioned oven, then stand by to gauge the timing for producing a golden brown surface. At a carefully calculated moment, I grasped the handle on the heavy oven door and lowered it, bracing myself against the blast of heat radiating from the open oven. Then came the critical moment: carefully turning over each piece of toast by hand before reinserting the shelves and browning the toast on the second side. Rudy warned me, "At some point, you're going drop that rack. Every toast girl does it at some point. They drag it out too fast, and everything spills all over the floor." His wicked grin indicated that the kitchen crew found that amusing. I silently vowed that this would not happen on my watch, and I felt enormous pride in making sure it never did.

There was also the business of "buttering" the toast. I am unsure it was butter, but something yellowish and melted stood in a #10 size can with a paint brush lodged inside, ready for applying the slippery stuff over the bread. Most toast girls found that by working very fast at the beginning of their shift, they could slather enough toast with the liquid to allow them to punch out early. They left the toast sinking into a soggy tired slump in the serving trays. This offended my ideal of "crisp buttered toast" and I began pacing my toasting to be in time with demand. I was rewarded for this extra care when a young man approached me one morning at the end of the semester. "I could always tell when you were the one on duty, because the toast was still crisp," he said. That appreciative remark was ample reward for the effort it had cost me. I felt pride in providing top quality for the group in "lower."

It is not accidental that all of these early work experiences involved working with my hands. There is a saying, "you can tell how a monk prays by the way he sweeps the cloister." For Benedictine monks, physical labor is an integral part of their training in a life of simplicity and meaning. *Ora et labora*—prayer and work—is the signature of the daily rhythm in their lives as they seamlessly move between baking bread and praying the psalms.⁶

I was ignorant of these connections between work and prayer in my youth, but I see now that I was shaped by my work experiences. I can piece together the strands of my early history and see my work in new terms, how I was offering refreshment to strangers, turning scraps—not wasting material—into objects of interest, taking special care to preserve quality in serving others, feeling the harmony and flow of coordinated team work. It was better preparation than I realized for a time when I would seek to imitate Brother Lawrence in the "practice of the presence of God."⁷ I could understand how his work and prayer flowed into each other as he went about his tasks in the scullery. I had experienced a life close to the ground, living by the work of my hands.

ENTERING THE WORLD OF WORK
Graduation from college connotes for most students the time to step into the "real world." Some of what we mean by that is independence from the family pocketbook. This would not be a big break for me, since our family's pocketbook was pretty thin, and I had felt an earthy connection to my environment—not only through the physical jobs I held, but also in the way I conceived of my relationship to God. My experience as a teenager in Pioneer Girls camp and club had introduced me to a concept that formed my philosophy of life while very young: "Christ in every phase of a girl's life."⁸ The underlying meaning rippled out in the way we conducted camp—at the waterfront, on the hiking trail, around the campfire, singing in the dining hall. God was present—incarnate, embodied, a pulsing energy in everything we did. Spiritual life was not confined to Bible study, which we called "exploration." It resonated throughout the day. As I faced the world of work after college, I felt impelled to find work that would make that same kind of connection between body and soul, heart and head. I knew what I wanted. With patience, I trusted it would come to me.

My expectation, as I approached graduation from college, was that I would find work that could establish me independently in my profession of Christian Education. Although Wheaton, like all colleges, tried to be helpful in providing leads for promising jobs within each major field, Christian Education was relatively new in the 1950s. I was graduating in an era before openings were plentiful. My advisor regretfully presented the one slender possibility she had in her files—teaching Bible classes in the Virginia school system, which still provided "released time" for this on an optional basis during the school day. It sounded dull to me, so when I was recommended for one of these rare openings, I turned it down. A second one was offered, and I refused that as well. I could not picture myself standing primly dressed in skirt, blouse, and heels in front of a class of restless kids, seated in bleak rows of desks nailed to the floor, and trying to sustain their interest for the requisite fifty minutes of released time, before I'd have to scurry off to another school in the district to repeat the same lesson to yet another class.

I had been bitten by a livelier kind of bug: my enthusiastic participation in Pioneer Girls camps. I had risen within the ranks of leadership each summer. I had been singled out for special opportunities—one of them, joining a summer-long team of camp counselors traveling across the Midwest, training leaders and leading camp activities. I had also held a volunteer leadership position on my college campus, preparing other students to lead clubs in surrounding towns. The organization was young and vibrant. Its well-articulated philosophy captivated me as a teenager—integrating all of life with giving glory to God and avoiding the stodginess and stiltedness of much church-sponsored religious education. Being part of it felt like play.

My heart was set on working at Pioneer Girls, so I did not apply anywhere else. By August, I had succeeded in turning down everything offered me. Then one day, I pulled a letter out of the mailbox bearing the familiar name and logo, "Pioneer Girls." I was overjoyed.

It was an offer. I began in the position of Publications Director. Although the title was grand, the job required the most rudimentary skills along with the more advanced knowledge acquired in my college major. After writing program materials, it fell to me to type the stencils, then run them off on the mimeograph machine, collate the pages and fold them, stuff them into envelopes I helped address, stamp and seal; and finally it sometimes became my task to lug them across the street to the post office. I joked that then I must go home and read them myself!

Through the next sixteen years I transitioned through a series of posts: Field Representative in the Rocky Mountains, National Camp Secretary commissioned to write a camp counselor manual, Program Division Director with a staff of seventeen including freelance writers across the country, Program Director at the Leadership Training Center on Michigan's Upper Peninsula, and finally Overseas Program Coordinator training interns to develop girls' work in other parts of the world. Along the way, I returned to graduate school to earn a Master's degree in my field, writing my dissertation on "The Philosophy of Pioneer Girls." The work formed me professionally, socially, spiritually; reciprocally I was given the opportunity to put my mark on the program and philosophy of the organization. At core, it was a happy blend.

It was a wild ride, full of ecstatic highs and warm associations with likeminded peers. It eventually descended into some bleak lows as the organization grew. Some of my distress was personal, centered on my struggles to mature emotionally and spiritually. At the same time the organization was going through growing pains as we entered the 1960s. New leadership was hired at the top, with resulting conflict trickling down through the lower echelons. The turbulent culture of the times influenced the organization to make defensive moves that felt out of sync with the direction I was going. I was becoming attuned to the larger culture—both Christian and secular. The board was concerned with the loss of finances that might result if we adopted a more progressive stance on issues like race. The board members became more intrusive, threatening the integrity of some of the principles the staff embraced. When their decisions began to impact me directly, I was not sure I fit any longer.

Disillusionment set in, and I began to think about leaving. Characteristically, my motto—"when in doubt, go to school"—provided an escape valve, and I registered at the University of Chicago for a PhD program in Sociology under the guise of pursuing my interest in cross-cultural work overseas. But inside I knew I was headed elsewhere. I just did not know where.

By the end of my tenure at Pioneer Girls in 1966 at the age of 36, I had yet to fill out an application or go on a job interview. This would be an unusual case, the exception to the rule, if my experience had stopped with this one example. But the pattern continued. From that point on, I would either find ways to create my work, or my network of friends and colleagues would generate invitations to participate in some project of interest when I needed part-time employment to support myself.

EXPERIENCES PREPARING ME FOR LIFE/WORK DIRECTION
For the next thirteen years until my arrival in Boston in 1979, a cluster of influences shaped me in radically new ways. These experiences evolved naturally, and in retrospect, I see how essential each one was in preparing me for what lay ahead in Boston—the formation of Life/Work Direction and my own life work within that ministry.

Social and Political Awareness
The years spent in graduate school at the University of Chicago during the turbulent decades of the sixties and seventies were mind-bending. I was a latecomer to political and social awareness. Although the inception

of Pioneer Girls had occurred in major cities with ethnic and racial diversity—Chicago, Detroit, Toronto, Boston, Los Angeles, New York City and northern New Jersey—the organization quickly followed the trend of evangelical churches in the fifties as they gravitated to the suburbs. At the time I left the organization, racial tensions were felt in some areas, such as our nonsegregated camps. I could see the handwriting on the wall—that Pioneer Girls' largely conservative constituency would not readily respond to the challenges posed by the civil rights movement.

Attending the University and living on Chicago's South Side, I was located in the middle of racial tensions and in contact with fellow students much more radical in their attitudes. I found several outlets for my raised consciousness. I started teaching a Sunday School class in a biracial church in the blighted Woodlawn area bordering the University. I participated in sponsoring a national conference on race for concerned evangelicals. I joined a small biracial group of ministers and others in ongoing "Conversations on the City" where we supported one another in staying in the city when many white churches fled to the suburbs as the racial mix in city neighborhoods changed. And finally, when a small group of us conceived of starting the Urban Life Center, a residential program for college students, a major component of the program had to do with raising the consciousness of white Christian college students by introducing them to persons of color who were willing to talk about their experience of life in the inner city. During this period, I was focused on what spiritual writers call "the active life." I was not yet tuned to the inner contemplative dimension, nor did I know its terminology.

Exploring the Inner Life

It was not just the times—the turmoil in the country over racial unrest and the war in Vietnam. It was my own inner clock that needed to be reset. Something needed to happen at the core of my personal life, my sense of who I was. As competent and successful as I may have appeared in that impressive string of job titles in Pioneer Girls, the inner reality was wobbly and unsatisfied at the core. I lived in a fairly small and enclosed world within Christendom, where I could easily "pass" as an able professional in ministry. I did not heed the more basic questions about my identity or my sexuality, if any one raised them with me.

Thomas Merton, a major articulator of the character of the inner life, is one of many writers in the contemplative tradition who insists on the connection between the psychological exploration of one's self and the coming to know and love God in intimacy.[9] I had never done this kind of inner work—exploring the unconscious compulsions that drove me, nor plumbing the extent of the self-deception that made me think I was happy. Secretly, I longed to marry, but I had repressed and denied my sexuality, wearing a pious Christian cover of acceptance of my single state. The usual avenues of change presented to me in my Christian milieu seemed to promise that there were clear spiritual answers that I had missed. The God I knew and preached to others promised abundant life and joy. But inside I was desperate.

My best friend at the time, Char Smith, was training to become a therapist, so our conversations together took a decidedly psychological turn. At one point, she gently suggested I consider therapy. I was initially resistant, but in 1967, I took the plunge. An intensive six months with a caring therapist helped me address the surface issues—shame about my body and its capacity for feminine sexuality, and the resulting distorted hatred of myself. The transformation was huge: "I was born again!" The change occurred rapidly, for I was "prepared ground"— prepared in part by the measure of my desperation, and by my tentative explorations of the psychological domain that opened me to the therapeutic mode. Also I stubbornly hung onto a faint hope that God was at work in my life. This made it possible for me to yield quickly to the therapeutic process.

Opening to Sexuality and Marriage

As a logical outcome of my therapy, I opened my arms and heart to the possibility of marriage, and to men who suddenly became available for friendship and romance. A year later, I met Don Schatz, a Jewish artist and poet who was surprised to find a woman on the University of Chicago campus who had a rocklike faith. It did not take him long to gravitate toward the circle of friends in a Bible study I was attending, and soon we were talking about marriage.

Meeting Don was a little bit of a miracle in itself. Although I was very intentional about seeking marriage, Don had a totally different mindset.

> *While traveling to Europe in 1962, I had a religious experience on the Isle of Majorca one day in a cathedral, and that set me on a spiritual quest. When I came back home to America, I started visiting the Trappist Abbey in Gethsemani to see if I had a vocation as a monk.*
>
> *On one visit, Thomas Merton came up to my room to talk about some of my drawings I had brought with me. He was a giant presence. But I did not see how my vocation fit into the life of a monk.*
>
> *I had no interest in dating. If I showed interest in a woman, it would be for marriage.*

Don began working as a research assistant to a Psychology professor at the University of Chicago while I was a graduate student. We would pass each other casually in the hallways, or in the elevator on his way down to the coffee machine in the basement. A few times I was a guinea pig for some of the research experiments he performed for his professor. The research project required Don to measure "pupil dilation and its relation to interest" while the research subject watched a film. But Don was measuring something else, as the months rolled by. He detected something special in me, but could not identify what it was. Miraculously, a chance stumble on my part one day catapulted us into a momentous encounter. I needed his rescue from a dilemma of my own making and he responded obligingly. We wound up sitting in a South Shore café eating a Reuben sandwich and drinking a coke on a sunny October afternoon in 1968. Love was stirring in us both. We began being together from that moment on. He explained:

I wanted someone to be my friend and not someone who would have a critical relationship to me, like my parents and others I knew. I tested the boundaries during those weeks and found Eunice was my equal in her confidence and sense of herself.

The day before we got married, Don was baptized in an African American Baptist church on Chicago's West Side. This epochal moment stands etched in time and memory as the culmination of Don's long quest for meaning as an artist and a person. He describes it in his characteristically oblique way as "the move from modernism to postmodernism." I saw it as his moving away from tradition and the law into freedom and the spirit. Baptism in the name of the Father, Son, and Holy Spirit set him free.

We entered into marriage with courage and optimism. We were sure it must have been God who arranged our paths to cross, since otherwise the intersection of two such different people was unlikely.

Don went out and got his first job, working at a prestigious art gallery downtown two months before the wedding. It was the cultural expectation of his upbringing that he should provide for me. He said:

I had never worked before. I wasn't made for that kind of life. I enjoyed Eunice being happy. Making her happy was the tune I played, a core melody. My experience in the art world was what I had to give.

Soon after our marriage, Don and I fell quickly into working together. The Urban Life Center launched us into the first of three decades of partnership in work as well as life. At the Center, I brought sociological and psychological orientations, and Don his art. He commented:

Eunice and her friends were focused on civil rights. I was not. The friends to whom she introduced me in those first months of marriage had no urban sophistication, and were naïve about my interests. I could adapt by living on the surface of social interactions.

They were idealists. They were not alone in this in the 1970s; this was also true of movements like New Age, Hippies and Yuppies.

I left the Frumkins Art Gallery job and began hanging out at the Urban Life Center. It was a rich, meaningful learning experience. I felt I could live on a different plane, evaluating students' artistic attempts without probing into the world of high art as I knew it. I was no longer painting. I became practical, used a common language. I wanted to encourage students to be self-directed in their art, to find their own voice.

In retrospect, I see that the Urban Life Center was more suited to my vocation than to Don's. Yet, he left a profound mark on the students with his refreshingly original and provocative challenges. Some may have thought that I had hitched my wagon to a star, but others thought it was more like a cyclone. At any rate, my story and Don's are inextricably linked. The pattern of working together would continue on several fronts: he joined me in teaching classes at universities in Chicago and Boston, and our partnership would culminate in the formation of Life/Work Direction. Working together as a married couple feels natural to us, and we recognize that it poses distinct blessings and challenges—both for us as a couple and for those who work with us. We influence each other deeply and can work harmoniously, and at the same time we cherish the free expression of our independent strengths. It is the story of our marriage. It is a vital part of what we would give to Life/Work Direction as well.

Don and Eunice Schatz still in love 41 years later

Attunement to the Psychological Dimension of my Calling

One area where I differ from Don is my interest in therapy. I experimented with a deepened form of therapy called bioenergetics that attuned me to the body's place in carrying emotional expressiveness, and led to my experimentation with work in clay, participation in "creative movement" and enjoying dance for the first time. My activities in these realms climaxed in my participation in a yearlong training program for Group Facilitators. I discovered I had gifts in using my psychological insight in my interactions with others as individuals and in groups. I was now defining myself in a particular sector of educational work previously unknown to me, one that coincided with my natural psychological bent and which would serve me well in my future work in Boston. I respected my own interior growth process, and I had experienced transformation in my own life. I wanted to help others unearth their true selves in all their authenticity and complexity.

Contact with National Issues through Conference Planning
Soon after completing my Master's degree in Sociology (pursuing the PhD no longer interested me), I was offered a job as a conference planner for a national organization attempting to use its influence within the realms of business and government. An enterprising man, John Naisbitt (best known for his first book, *Megatrends*) had started Urban Research Corporation with funding from Goldman Sachs based on the idea of collating newspaper stories and providing them in a timely fashion to businesses. He conceived of a supporting Conference Department that would bring in experts on topics of current interest for a three-day colloquium, transcribe the presentations and discussion and sell it. I was part of a three-person team setting up the conferences. My identification here was not with the job, but the part of it that nourished me—the stimulation coming from the movers and shakers of society in such fields as law, educational technology, and government. I enjoyed the experience with a feeling of subtle detachment, since most of my daily energy was soon absorbed in the shaping of the Urban Life Center. After a brief stint full-time, I worked as consultant, running a few national conferences with an accomplished colleague until the organization's funding fizzled out.

Teaching in Higher Education
In the fall of 1970, Urban Life Center got its start. Don and I were two of the twelve founding board members. In order for the Center to grant students college credit for their semester with us, we needed to secure academic credentials. Initially, we affiliated with Roosevelt University as one of their experimental outposts for nontraditional students. It turned out that I could teach at the Center as an adjunct Roosevelt University professor with Don adding "spice and intellectual heft" to our classroom discussions. The post provided us steady part-time income through our remaining years in Chicago.

This professional connection in higher education would serve me well as a link to academia when I moved to Boston. My focus was on experiential education, a field that fit with my own academic training and personal philosophical proclivities. To me, learning occurred through doing, rather than being told. It had been the case in Pioneer Girls, and it was core to our orientation in guiding students at the Urban Life Center as they experienced the complex urban environment with its layers of race and class, its art and architecture, its variety of forms of religious expression.

A Predisposition to Non-bureaucratic Organization
One other thread in the strands of my life in those Chicago years is worth mentioning. At one point, I took a professional job in a major bureaucratic institution—the highly-regarded American Hospital Association. I had written for a health education project in one of my patchwork part-time jobs. The supervisor who hired me thought I would be a good fit for a permanent position at the American Hospital Association where she worked. I decided to try it out at a time when the Urban Life Center was not yet able to support me financially. The salary AHA quoted was twice as much as anything I had ever made. I was soon to learn that high pay could be accompanied by unpleasant bureaucratic constraints against which I would immediately chafe.

My first clue was the two weeks of training just to prepare for working there, getting my identification, and being subject to God knows what kind of background checks. I was being groomed to be an "AHA Person," I now see. On my first day there, I was chagrined to find that secretaries ate in one dining area, and those of us on professional staff ate in another place. I deliberately chose to be with the secretaries. Then, on my fourth day, I wore a pants suit to work. Alas, this was considered radical attire, a subversive insertion of latent feminism. I was discreetly and definitely informed of my gaffe. I saw that I would be more welcome wearing mini skirts like the secretaries.

One day in my second week, I had enough. I called Don, tearful and in misery. Characteristically, he responded, "Why don't you leave?"

"Leave? Leave? Leave!" I could l e a v e. . . ? I gathered my files together, as if to go to the library—a routine privilege accorded me—and went home. Next day, I went in and resigned. Finally, I was free again. I spent not one moment in regret over the lost pay.

That experience was a blip on the radar screen of my life. My focal point was always on our involvement with the Urban Life Center, initially as volunteers and eventually as full-time staff. After two years, we became co-directors in title, while relying on an active board for practical support in carrying on the activities of the Center.

Doors Open for Change
The Urban Life Center stabilized organizationally during the 1970s. When Scott Chesebro and his wife joined us in 1977, Don and I saw an opportunity to take a three-month sabbatical in 1978 to consider our options. We had become restless in our roles and were ready for change, even a major transition that would involve a geographic move.

An entry in my journal, written before leaving Chicago, may have been prescient in anticipating a deeper current of movement than I knew how to articulate.

Will I find my new future in some exploration of self, rather than service to society? Is this the deeper, more daring trip? I am taught that it is weaker, escapist, self-centered. I must be very sure before I embark on this Second Journey.

"The images and symbols of our minds introduce us to a wider world than that of our actual historic life." Perhaps some answers will come to me through the life of the imagination as I set my sails, and remain open to the winds that blow. Winds of the Spirit. Winds of my dreams.

When I wrote those lines, I thought—as most people do—that transitions are a move upward, borne by those "winds of the Spirit." I had not yet grasped the essential truth that an inner journey always begins by a movement down. The downward spiral that was occurring in my outer life in Dorchester was a necessary precedent before I would be ready to embark on a more interior "Second Journey."

Right now the interior path was on hold; I needed work and a paycheck.

CHAPTER 5

Experiencing the Job Search:
making choices

1979-1980

I HAD ALWAYS FOUND MY WAY INTO WORK, either creating it or through connections provided by a network of friends and colleagues. Until Boston. Suddenly I no longer had a ready-made network to pull me along into the next phase of my life. My security lay in my trust that I could find a way into the field I identified as *life work planning*.

I came alive to the job search. I could embark on it according to the protocol Bolles laid out so ably in his *Parachute* book. I did my research carefully, using the resources available in those pre-Internet days. "Temping" was a way to earn quick cash, and if used judiciously, could be more broadly useful. A Chicago friend steered me to a temp firm in Boston that specialized in placing college-degreed women in jobs, presumably catering to businesses in a city loaded with institutions that valued an extra dollop of sophistication and intelligence.

So I applied there and began getting out into the city, feeling its pulse, ascending the escalators to the corridors of power, looking back down on the city from the heights of corporate headquarters and banks. But not all the temp jobs rose to the level of challenge the temp firm advertised, so I became more selective, choosing jobs that promised better access to my interests, such as university-related jobs.

I knew it was wise to keep more than one track going and prepared three résumés, only one of which pointed toward life work planning.

A second suggested my ability to coordinate conferences since I had gained experience in that field. The third focused on my involvement in non-traditional higher education through the Urban Life Center and part-time teaching at Roosevelt University in Chicago. I began to ace out innovative programs in higher education in Boston favoring the "nontraditional student," usually seen then as women and other minorities lacking a traditional college degree, but rich in life experience and full of untapped potential.

I visited Northeastern University to investigate a new program geared especially toward women, including a career assessment component. I dropped in at the office of the new program to inquire. When I told the person at the front desk a bit about my own interests and background, she immediately called in the Dean to talk with me. Even though my purpose had been simply to gain information by networking, I was alert to the opportunity to take full advantage of this key contact. The Dean was congenial and interested. He proceeded to ask me all the usual interview questions. Essentially, he hired me then and there to teach evening classes in Self Assessment and Career Development as an adjunct professor. All I needed to do was file a resumé and references.

Taking this as a part-time job was a significant step, even though I was still searching for full-time work. Although I did not yet know it, I would need the protection of this partial income while I moved toward my unknown future. It was a familiar pattern for me—patching together a work life so that I could be free to center my energies on what I loved, supporting myself with little "gigs" around the fringes.

One day soon after this, I spied a temp opening in an organization I had already taken note of because of its specialization in helping women enter the labor force. It was headed by Renée Levine, author of the aptly titled book *How To Get a Job in Boston*.[10] I could not have asked to be in a more central position in my chosen field in Boston. Renée recommended that I apply for the job of career counselor in a government-funded program held at a YWCA storefront in downtown Framingham, working with women trying to move from welfare to work. This sounded like something that fit me—conducting a program for women, with the responsibility and freedom to develop my own curriculum.

※

At the YWCA job interview, I was asked a string of questions about my background and experience. Could I lead groups? *I had a year's professional training in group work.* Could I develop a curriculum for the class I was to teach? *I had been an educator all my life, and loved the process of putting methods and materials together.* Could I counsel women of all ages? *Those sixteen years in an all-female organization training women leaders passed this test amply.* Could I work with varying socio-economic levels? *I taught Sunday School in the inner city, and had participated in research at the University of Chicago in Adult Basic Education, a program for minority women lacking literacy skills.* The interviewer prodded and probed every facet of the requisite skills desired for this position; my experience not only matched the qualifications; sometimes it outstripped them.

The interviewer had no good reason not to hire me, except that now she worried that with all this experience, I might not be willing to accept the modest pay. I would later discover that expectations of high pay were characteristic of Boston, perhaps due to the influence of several prestigious universities turning out a crop of graduates with correspondingly demanding needs for recognition and compensation.

Apologetically, she told me the salary was just $12,000 a year. I didn't gasp or flinch. I just looked her straight in the eye and told her, "Yes, the salary is fine." Inside I was overjoyed. Twelve thousand dollars a year felt ample to support the lifestyle to which Don and I had become accustomed ever since our marriage. Money never ranked high on my list of values. For me, work had been play. The money was a bonus, and the fact that it was often low in comparison to parallel organizations carried no stigma for me. My criteria for job satisfaction were different.

By summer, I memorized the most efficient route from Dorchester to Framingham, placing my ruler on the map and charting my way down side streets and over hill and dale. It turned out to be a sylvan route for the most part, with fewer stop signs and traffic lights. I now know it is a back route lots of people know, but back then I took peculiar pride in mapping a labyrinthine way on my own.

Inside the YWCA storefront where clusters of women convened each day, I set to work creating an atmosphere conducive to learning. I scheduled a workday for a Saturday, and recruited other staff to join me in rearranging the furniture in a friendlier constellation. We rolled up our sleeves to paint the walls canary yellow, and plastered colorful posters everywhere. A giant safe loomed large against one wall, and since it had to remain there, one of my helpers grinned wickedly and suggested, "Let's camouflage it with this brilliant lime green paint!" With that finishing touch, I was ready for my first group of women.

Week after week through the seasons, in trooped groups of five or six women at a time for a six-week workshop where we set upon the task of exploring their readiness for work, their appreciation of their abilities, and their understanding of how to present themselves to a prospective employer. In addition to the practical stuff, we talked about life issues. Most of them were single parents, having small children at home. Many of them had never planned a budget. Most were unsure of themselves when it came to entering the corporate world of the big high tech firms that were located nearby and ready to hire entry-level workers.

Coming from my own recent experience of hitting the skids economically, I resonated easily with these women in a way I could not have years before. We sat around the table and laughed and cried and told stories, and listened to one another. Staff in the outer office used to kid me, hearing hoots of laughter emanating from the back room. "What are you doing in there?" I did not apologize for the noise. I knew women were coming to life, and I felt a part of it.

So I now could chalk this one up, right? I'd come to Boston, was unemployed, and I found a job. End of story?

※

Something was not quite enough for me in this job. Was it the tenuousness of being supported by a federal grant? I recognized that such a resource is capricious at best, depending on the current political mood. Was it the awkward split between our humble little storefront located in downtown Framingham—on "the other side of the tracks"—and the more splendid headquarters of the West Suburban YWCA north of town in a quiet meadowland? The women streaming in and out of that headquarters building were just as deserving of attention as the women I was meeting downtown, but these were women with the leisure to pursue their interests in their free time, while their husbands supported them, working in those fast-growing technology firms on Route 128. I was unsure that the whole picture of the YWCA would be a congenial environment for me long term. Whatever the reason, I sensed that I was destined for something closer to my heart, though I did not yet know exactly where I might find it or what it would ultimately look like.

Even more important, coming home to Don every day, and sharing stories, I found he was restless. He had come to Boston determined to pursue his work as a poet and an artist. Connecting with an art community in Boston was not easy. He ventured out into the city, checking out resources for his interests. He even considered enrolling in Mass College of Art for an advanced degree, but an interview with a faculty member discouraged him from pursuing his art through that route. "You're beyond that," he told Don. "Going to school would be a waste of your time." He sensed that Don needed a different kind of stimulus and environment.

The world of higher education was familiar to both of us because of our positions at the Urban Life Center, and Boston was an academic Mecca. One of our first contacts in Boston had been with the Mennonite community in Cambridge composed of professors and graduate students who clustered together to maintain their primal ties with one another while occupying positions of influence in academic professions. But we did not see our way leading into this world either.

Don was also influenced by what made me happy. Marrying a woman of thirty-nine years of age meant connection to a person who had lived two decades as an independent professional. This, plus my commitment to Christian work, denoted stability and a willingness to live by faith. Don watched me move into the YWCA job with both curiosity and detachment. He came out to the Y with me several times to psych out my world and quickly sensed that it would not hold me long term. He knew that the governmental bureaucratic framework did not fit my temperament. He was caught, as I was, in a living situation among the dispossessed that was alien to us, and in the midst of a city that boasted world-famous institutions of higher learning, beating with a different pulse than ours.

Seeing me in action, he entertained the possibility that the two of us might find a way in Boston to partner in some work. After all, his original impetus for our work at the Urban Life Center had been for a "Christian Center for the Arts." The end product had turned in a more sociological direction. It was thinkable that there might be a way that his interests and mine could mesh in Boston, and that thereby he could find a way to move into society just as he had helped young college students do in the past.

Don went on a quest to find an arts community in Boston in the faint hope he might find some Christians pursuing the arts in ways that probed deeper than caricature or maudlin expression or as a tool of propaganda. Several people he questioned told him about a group of Christians in downtown Boston that had some interest in the arts. It was an ecumenical venture called Many Mansions. Don decided to pay them a visit, unaware of how much was waiting for us in this exploration.

PART TWO

Forming a Work that Endures

weaving the story of Life/Work Direction

"It is by God's mercy that we are engaged in this ministry."
II Corinthians 4:1

CHAPTER 6

Many Mansions:
finding a starting point to weave

1980-1981

Downtown Boston had charmed us from the moment we arrived in the city—the ancient Commons flanked by the gold-domed State House on one side, Park Street Church with its lighted spire on another, and the Episcopal Cathedral on the third. Two subway lines intersected below the surface, one of them the Red Line that connected us from our home in Dorchester to Don's job in Cambridge. In my first weeks in town, I walked around Boston's quaint downtown area like a visiting tourist, camera strapped to my shoulder. The Commons provided me with plenty of photographic material: an old sea skipper carving wood, a tall skinny juggler entertaining the crowds, mothers with strollers and small children, vagrants sleeping off the chill of a homeless night, families riding the swan boats that sailed on the limpid pond in the adjacent Public Gardens. Something about the lighting in early morning or late afternoon caught my eye. I experienced Boston as a stranger, and I fell in love.

It was a scant half block from the Commons that Don found the Many Mansions enterprise in a five-story building wedged between a Chinese bookstore and a convent selling religious icons. Two doors away stood the Brattle Book Shop, legendary for its selection of rare used books. Don could begin to feel at home in this environment.

Don walked through the arched entrance into the midst of chaotic reconstruction. Young men and women in overalls were full of energy as they pounded down partitions, climbed ladders and perched on scaffolding, armed with buckets of plaster. They were tearing out walls and counters and shelves in order to turn the first floor of the old shoe store into a restaurant. A rickety elevator took Don to the third floor where the Many Mansions offices were located. He was greeted with effusive friendliness by an assortment of volunteers—two suburban homemakers bustling over preparations for the noon meal and another struggling with an archaic addressograph machine. The two co-directors, Dick Faxon and an associate, Richard Valantasis, both Episcopal priests, stepped forward to introduce themselves.

It was almost lunch time, but first noonday prayers were conducted in a swept-out corner of the third floor, where a makeshift altar stood before a row of windows looking out over rooftops of nearby buildings and onto an alley. A few chairs were placed facing the altar. The rest of the group sat on low shoe store stools salvaged from the first floor. A gong sounded to announce the commencement of quiet before one of the volunteers read the "daily office" from *The Book of Common Prayer*.

Lunch took place around an enormous square table on which women placed a huge wooden bowl of salad and a tureen of soup. Conversation was lively, as Don tried to sniff out just who these persons were who had gathered from city and suburbs to join in this anomalous enterprise. Richard Valantasis found out Don was interested in the arts and began plying him with questions. Don gave him a copy of his latest work, "Jew for Jesus," written in Chicago. Richard was intrigued and began trying to convince Don to join them in their outreach at Many Mansions.

Don began hanging out at Many Mansions. He would sit at the piano in the chapel and play, and once he brought in his bass fiddle to play with a musically talented visitor who happened by. An empty space on the second floor was designated for various programs, including possibly an art gallery—an idea with a familiar ring for Don. Was Many Mansions a place where he might pursue some of his interest in the arts with a congenial community of peers?

He was welcomed warmly and given a key to the building. He soon found that the role available to him entailed bookkeeping and other administrative tasks for which he was not well suited. But the conversations with people intrigued him. Something about the spirit of the place and people resonated—a combination of religious fervor, and a hint of familiarity with the art world.

Slowly Don began to discover that Many Mansions had less to do with the arts than he had been told. He found that it was an ecumenical venture, largely evangelistic in purpose, geared toward the unchurched. A group of persons from several traditions—Catholics, Baptists, Episcopalians, and others—had been meeting together informally in downtown Boston for several months to pray. They had no permanent location and their goals were modest. As part of their outreach, they envisioned using the arts in some way, principally through music.

In the process of looking for a meeting place, a five-story building on West Street came onto the market in 1979. Dick Faxon instantly recognized its strategic location—at the intersection of the financial district, the Commons, the theatre district, and city, state and federal government offices. Of the group that had been meeting for prayer for several months, Dick stood in the best position to take advantage of this unforeseen opportunity to locate a center in downtown Boston. He had recently received an inheritance after the death of his father and offered part of it to make the acquisition of this building in a prime downtown location possible. Modest goals suddenly expanded to match the size of the building; the name "Many Mansions" was chosen to fit the enlarged vision.

What might they do with five floors? Don watched from the sidelines warily as he listened to the core group begin envisioning a restaurant on the first floor—something to draw people in off the streets, and a fitting setting for Saturday night "cafés" where musicians might perform in a contemporary style, softening people for an evangelistic appeal. The second floor had convenient space for seminars and sessions for business people working in the financial sector nearby, where they could meet for discussion and prayer as they looked for ways to relate their work to their faith. The third floor was suitable for offices and contained space for a chapel where light streamed through floor-to-ceiling windows. Dick proposed that the fourth and fifth floors be renovated into residences for persons such as "policemen and social workers"—providing a sense of community in the middle of the congestion of the inner city. It was like Dick to think of all these tiers of society gathered around a common focus.

This impulsive move into the West Street building on the part of the founding group generated new enthusiasm. Young persons were eager to participate in the renovation—tearing down walls, clearing out construction debris. High unemployment in the early 1980s left lots of people available. Soon the place was crawling with youthful energy.

The sudden increase in size of the project carried complications with it, however. It created a split from the original vision of Many Mansions as a not-for-profit ministry supported by donations. The expansion that flowed from occupying this larger building in a prime downtown location put the restaurant in the uncomfortable position of being run as a for-profit business providing the main source of income to support the ministry. This turned everything on its head, giving undue prominence to the business side of the venture. It would prove a fatal flaw.

A for-profit restaurant in downtown Boston would present legal and bureaucratic hurdles. An interminable governmental process was required to secure the permissions to renovate the building according to code. Ever since the famous Coconut Grove fire decades earlier, Boston installed exceedingly stringent fire safety regulations. The people gathered for Many Mansions' ministry were unaware of these legal tangles. The younger people gravitated more naturally to the familiar aspects of restaurant management and experience: table size, décor, and menus. They could see a meaningful place for themselves as employed staff of the restaurant and café.

Richard Valantasis stepped into the role of manager of the restaurant and began digging into his own Greek heritage to come up with finger-licking recipes. Always a man who functioned with flair, he set to work optimistically. He ordered printed stationery for the restaurant—reams we would use as scrap paper long after the dream of the restaurant died. He ordered bolts of crimson and yellow cloth, presumably for tablecloths and to festoon the bare brick walls and add color. I still have yards of it in our closet.

※

Don observed this development of events as he visited in his spare time. After a few weeks, he began urging me to come down and visit too. "They need you," he told me. He really liked the people but wondered about the viability of what was envisioned. He knew how important it was that I find something in Boston to which I could say a hearty "Yes." So I dropped by one day to check it out. Dick greeted me warmly and quickly intuited that I had energy and skills to contribute and invited the two of us to take part. Don and I realized this was an opportunity for us to work together again, but we worried that Many Mansions was out of kilter with the way both of us thought and functioned in our religious lives. Its focus was evangelism, and at that time we were still the "unchurched" that Many Mansions' brochure claimed to want to reach. The leadership of priests both Catholic and Episcopal—and the resultant subtly hierarchical atmosphere, was foreign to us. We were in the midst of lay people who addressed the leadership as "Father" with almost reverential tones. There was another element was missing for me: attention to the psychological dimension of spiritual growth, a strong interest of mine.

On a practical level, Don and I had some hesitancy about linking our futures to this project. My visit to Many Mansions had confirmed for Don that what he felt was also what I saw, and I could articulate it. We knew how possession of a large building could choke the elemental vision of a ministry and sap its energy, diverting it to the needs of the physical structure and the consequent costs. It had happened to us at the Urban Life Center in its first two years. Yet, we felt strangely drawn to the people we met at Many Mansions. I was aware that a critical mass of young persons had come together here concerned about the very issues of life and work to which I was prepared to devote my energies at this stage in my life. Not tangentially, it took us away from our difficult living environment and into a world more familiar to us.

Chief among the persons we met at Many Mansions was Dick Faxon himself, who had clearly sacrificed the most for his vision. He had told us enough of his own story to create a sympathetic bond, and we felt inclined to join him as helpers despite the lack of clarity of the venture.

Dick's religious journey was a colorful tapestry interwoven by several strands. His roots in the Episcopal Church were strong, but he combined this with a large dose of empathy for the warmth and vitality of evangelical Protestant groups and charismatic movements that had a profound effect on the way in which he carried his faith day to day. He placed great importance on the ecumenical nature of his venture; his affinity with Roman Catholics meant that it was natural for him to collaborate with Father Kevin at St. Anthony's Shrine located a few blocks from Many Mansions. The group that gathered at West Street included evangelicals from Protestant groups of every stripe, often from the suburbs, but also Catholic and Episcopal priests and congregants. I was fascinated by the blend of different traditions, exemplified in one instance by the near-parity in the gifts coming in big checks from affluent suburban Protestant donors and sacks of coins collected at mass at the Shrine from Catholic parishioners, most of them city dwellers of very modest means.

We stayed on the edges, tentatively feeling our way forward. In May of 1980, Dick Faxon formally asked us to come on staff for the summer, promising us a salary. We decided to take the leap.

Why did we say "yes" to Dick Faxon's offer? To this day, I do not fully understand why because it is so entangled in Don's and my marriage. We have often joked that each of us feels that the other one has the power in our decision-making. We are strongly influenced by each other.

Don thought there was something unique about the spirit he found at Many Mansions. He said:

> *I call it the fluidity of contrasts: rich and poor; the Catholics from St. Anthony's Shrine from Boston's ethnic conclaves and the suburban Episcopalians from Sudbury and Concord; evangelicals from Ruggles Street Baptist and Park Street Church, and the seminarians at Harvard Divinity School living in Harvard Square; the community activists from South Boston and the South End, and the recent graduates from Ivy League institutions with prep school backgrounds; a novice from a monastery and a lawyer in private practice. I saw a bright new world that was "other" than what I had been part of in the Midwest. But in the end, my decision to join the people at Many Mansions was all feelings.*

I would have to agree with the last statement for myself. I suppose that my familiarity with the evangelical world of Christendom, as well as an intellectual acquaintance with mainstream Protestantism, made me confident that I could find enough common ground with these disparate elements, but I didn't really know that at the outset. I saw that Don was open to the risk and I sensed there was a place for me, so when Dick invited us it was natural to say yes.

These impulses are never simple. In hindsight, I see why I was drawn to Dick Faxon. I was still grieving the death of my father. My dad was also a minister, a quiet contemplative sort, tender hearted and a wonderful father. Dick exuded the same spirit, allowing me to complete the grieving process as we began to work together.

Don's enthusiasm for the group was contagious, and we both had begun to care about what happened to the people gathered. I resigned from my job in Framingham, but prudently kept my part-time teaching at Northeastern University. Don had left his job at the Harvard Coop bookstore, and began to work at the Chinese bookstore next door to Many Mansions. We needed very little money to live, and actually wanted to live closer to the edge financially in order to have more freedom to pursue the unknown future we were sure God had in store for us. Would this enterprise be part of God's direction for our future? It didn't look promising at the moment, but we acted in blind trust.

❧

Even as the place was still abuzz with expectations and ideas, Dick understood that all was not well with the fundamentals of the project. He frequently came to work worried. He was the chief carrier of the vision; but the project relied on his initial investment more than was wise. Some of those around him were naïve about the implementation of the vision;

one person made a remark that indicated he thought Dick had a nearly endless supply of cash to infuse into the project if it faltered. The persons working there on clerical and administrative tasks—women from his former parish in Sudbury and others—were totally devoted to Dick and to the cause he espoused, but they were out of their depth in understanding the legal and financial perils arising.

Don and I sensed that underneath the surface enthusiasm, the daily prayer times in the chapel, the ebullient lunches around the rough wooden table at noon, the project was more fragile than outward appearances would indicate. While the workmen came in daily wearing their hard hats, beginning the task of renovation, there was an undercurrent of anxiety.

At the precise moment when Don and I agreed to begin working at Many Mansions for the summer, the project collapsed. Renovating the ancient building in accord with city fire safety codes for a restaurant was proving financially impossible. On a more basic organizational level, the mingling of ministry and business in a two-pronged mission was untenable. In addition, there proved to be a problem in getting a clear title to the building. Uncertainty was pervasive. In anguish over the crumbling of his vision, Dick called a meeting of the workmen and told them their work was terminated.

Dick Faxon in the final days at Many Mansions

It was as though Don and I had just stepped off a cliff into free fall. Remarkably, we had anticipated this turn of events, so instead of feeling let down, we were hopeful beyond any practical reason. We persevered, trusting that life would emerge from the death of a vision. We needed to build on a firmer base, one more in harmony with the concerns we held in common with Dick.

Richard Valantasis left shortly thereafter. Others would drift away more slowly. But not everyone. We focused our attention on the motley crew of remaining volunteers who made several attempts to resuscitate something of the original vision. A few "café" evenings were conducted at a nearby restaurant, Blazing Salads, thanks to owner Vicky Thomas, a member of St. Anthony's Shrine, who was sympathetic to Many Mansions' vision. There was modest turnout. Two plucky volunteers, Ann Stitt and Chris Waugh, decided to operate a sidewalk cart in front of the building in July—a custom of other downtown restaurants—offering lunch to passersby. It was hard for some to give up the dream of the restaurant, but when the cart proved to be a lot of work with minimal response, we let go of that part of the project.

During these months, Dick was engrossed in the difficult and intricate matters of closing down the operation called Many Mansions. He would never be able to receive the title to the building nor did he see a way to recoup his personal financial losses. Some members of his board were helpful in this; a few had abandoned the sinking ship. In addition, a new worry plagued Dick. It turned out that in the process of demolition, workers had been exposed to asbestos around the pipes. The threat of possible lawsuits lingered for several years before being resolved without incident.

One day Dick came to work wearing a neck brace, a sign of the tension he was carrying in his body as well as in his mind and soul. He could not help but see the project as a failure, and took personal responsibility for that, although this was far from the whole truth. He was a doggedly faithful man to the end, and we stood with him doing what we could to help bring the ship to port.

SUPPORTING THE UNEMPLOYED
The corps of young persons planning to work at Many Mansions were cast adrift but continued to show up out of affection for the community feeling generated there. When wintry winds blew through that old unheated building, we rented space next door over the Chinese bookstore where Don worked. The space looked enormous and bordered on the industrial in décor. We set to work transforming it into a welcoming place for people to gather—persons whose hopes for finding a place to serve at Many Mansions were now dashed. We set out the luxuriant array of plants women had contributed, and moved a slightly battered piano loaned by Dick into one corner. We kept the ubiquitous coffeepot bubbling and sending out its welcoming fragrance, as we grappled with the question of what we could do to respond in a practical way to those who lingered in our company.

My first spontaneous impulse was to conduct a Support Group for the Unemployed, and I enlisted Don's assistance in this. Judie Spitz, a woman who participated in one of my groups at the YWCA Women's

Resource Center in Framingham, had followed me to Many Mansions and was hanging out with me and the others there, intrigued by the energy and dedication of the folks assembled. She quickly identified the need of group members for something more substantive than support. "What these people need is a Workshop," she said. Dick welcomed the initiative. Together, Judie and I convened a pilot workshop. We never dreamed it would turn out to be the first of a long series of forty workshops led by Dick Faxon, Don and me. We began with a bare bones curriculum, predictive of a more elaborate design that would emerge out of our experience.

The very first person to join a workshop was a young man named Chris Waugh, who had left a lucrative job in computer programming in the Midwest to find a calling that would more directly connect with his relationship to Christ. He was in the process of weaning himself away from "a corporate man image."

Chris quit his job in Illinois and traveled through the country in his beat up Volkswagen, convinced that his lifestyle was "an insufficient expression of who I was in Christ." He made his way to New England and was a student for a while at Gordon-Conwell Theological Seminary. He became involved in a prison ministry at Deer Island, which he referred to as "a lynchpin in my life." He also served as choir director of a church in Boston. After a year of this, he said, "It was becoming clear that my vocation in Christ was not that of a selfless do-gooder, a suffering saint. I was trying to justify my own existence from the people I served, demanding that those I served enjoy it."

The workshop helped Chris see that he could do what he wanted—namely singing—and enjoy it. "Some might say that work is the sweat of your brow. I learned that work is a form of love." Singing expressed Chris at the deepest place of his being.

During his time in Boston, Chris found many ways to develop his considerable musical skill. One innovative adventure took him into the subways early mornings with two members of a madrigal singers group. They performed at Harvard Square, Downtown Crossing, and Government Center, singing for impatient commuters waiting for the subway. Chris now serves as cantor at his church in Quebec City, where he and his family live.

Chris and his fellow participants liked the workshop and told their friends who in turn begged for another. The second workshop was offered in January at the Shrine, then in rapid succession, we ran a third, and a fourth. It was at the fourth workshop that Scott Walker arrived as a participant. He had visited Many Mansions the previous summer, with his CUJ college student interns in tow. Now he appeared in order to meet his own needs for vocational direction, taking readily to our approach to life work exploration. He tells the story:

In Scott's Words

I followed a path of need and curiosity to the door of Many Mansions in downtown Boston. I was twenty-four at the time and riding the wave of post-college vision into pursuits that were both compelling and perplexing as I considered where they were leading me.

Little did I know then that the threads of my life and those of this organization would gradually be woven together. What I found was rare and vital.

I found regard for my *being* in relation to my *doing*. I was offered a place to stand back from the front lines of my pursuits (at that time in an inner-city ministry and church planting experience) to give attention to what I was learning about myself—what God was revealing in me, beneath the surface of the doings that could so easily preoccupy me. Here, mainly through the patient process of telling and reflecting on my life story, I began to recognize that my way of joyful service was in teaching.

I found a rich, collaborative perspective. My fellow pilgrims and I had the ear of three distinctly different people: Don and Eunice Schatz and Dick Faxon—a poet, an educator, and a priest—who had thrown their lots in together in mid-life to offer guidance to souls like me. The result was a full-bodied blend of perspective gathered not only through their different words and questions for me, but through the energetic give-and-take I witnessed between them. Apart from a common commitment to Jesus, there was no party line here but a diversity of insight that invited me to wonder about my own distinct nature and capacity for collaboration.

I found access through creative simplicity and community. It was 1981, a time of recession and high unemployment. Fees were kept low so that people like me who were between jobs or not making much in the first seasons of work exploration could afford to come.

LIFE/WORK DIRECTION INCORPORATES

Because the work attracted people like Scott and Chris, we could see the fire of enthusiasm had been ignited and was spreading. By February, it made sense for us to incorporate separately from Many Mansions as a legal not-for-profit corporation, chartered by the Commonwealth of

Massachusetts. We settled on the name "Life/Work Direction" and wrote a simple statement of purpose in the charter:

"To provide spiritual direction through an ecumenical context rooted in the historical Judeo-Christian tradition for persons wishing to integrate their faith with their whole life/work."

On February 12, 1981, the suggested Scripture reading for the day from *The Book of Common Prayer* ended with II Corinthians 4:12: "So now death is at work in us, *but life is at work in you,"* which confirmed our choice of a name. I could feel a new beginning, and it buoyed Dick's spirits considerably. A phoenix was rising from the ashes — a ministry that was characterized by the spirit of his humble approach to service. He was beginning to count on Don and me, and a spirit of community was forged between us that would endure.

COMING HOME TO A DORCHESTER STOREFRONT

We were now set upon a new path. We continued convening new workshops of five or six, as people requested them. By late spring, we knew the program was viable and began looking for affordable space for this fledgling ministry. This took us back to Dorchester, where a storefront two blocks from our home was available at a reasonable rate. On the afternoon of the annual Dorchester Day Parade in June 1981, we moved to Savin Hill Avenue. We constituted a triumphal procession, bearing old shoe store shelving and stools, an array of plants and beat-up desks and chairs, which had been given to Many Mansions. While we lugged the furniture inside, rows of Dorchester drill teams, war veterans and decorated floats passed by headed for a festive community celebration on Savin Hill beach nearby.

Dick was delighted that this storefront was on the Red Line allowing an easy commute from his home in Cambridge. He never complained despite occasional breakdowns on the T, which might leave him stuck in a tunnel. He also took great pleasure in settling into a neighborhood that included working people and families who were struggling or dispossessed. It was part of his character to refuse to take advantage of the privilege that came with his family's station in life.

Don and I felt that this move of the ministry close to home was redemptive for us. We had a comforting place to come each day right in our neighborhood, a reprieve from the harshness of our surroundings. A new life and work had begun.

CHAPTER 7

Laying a Foundation for a Life Work:
identifying warp threads

1981-1985

WE SETTLED INTO OUR NEW WORK WITH ZEST. Each evening, a stream of five or six persons came walking downhill from the Savin Hill T stop and entered our door, drawn inside by the aroma of a home-cooked meal. We were following the gracious custom begun at Many Mansions, where a lot of care was given to hospitality. It was natural to continue this as part of Life/Work Direction, preparing meals each evening before our workshops convened. Using a two-burner hot plate and an electric fry pan, we served heaping platters of rice or pasta adorned with colorful vegetables. A huge wooden bowl cradled a tossed salad. Dessert was made at our home nearby and carried in. Conversation around the table was lively as we ate, then quieted as we went into workshop mode for the next two-and-a-half hours with scarcely a break in momentum.

PUTTING DOWN ROOTS: THE CORE VISION
Three things are necessary in starting a new work: a good idea—a core vision rooted in values that can stand the test of time; good people—capable and committed to the vision; and a "critical mass" of persons responsive to the idea being offered. Others may start by thinking in terms of writing a grant proposal, securing funding, renting space, developing a board of directors, or writing a constitution, but that was the wrong approach for us.

Our common vision was expressed in the name we chose for the ministry: Life/Work Direction. Finding a direction for a life work is, at root, a spiritual task. The Scripture reading for Friday, February 27, the date we incorporated, expressed the spirit of our vision exactly, including the final phrase that put a benediction on our choice of a name:

Therefore, since it is by God's mercy that we are engaged in this ministry, we do not lose heart.

We renounce the hidden things of dishonesty, refusing to practice cunning or to falsify God's word; but by the open statement of the truth we commend ourselves to the conscience of everyone in the sight of God.

For we do not proclaim ourselves; we proclaim Jesus Christ as Lord and ourselves as your slaves for Jesus' sake.

For it is the God who said, "Let light shine out of darkness," who has shone in our hearts to give the light of the knowledge of the glory of God in the face of Jesus Christ.

But we have this treasure in clay jars, so that it may be made clear that this extraordinary power belongs to God and does not come from us.

We are afflicted in every way, but not crushed; perplexed, but not driven to despair; persecuted, but not forsaken; struck down, but not destroyed; always carrying in the body the death of Jesus, so that the life of Jesus may also be seen in us.

For while we live, we are always being given up to death for Jesus' sake, so that the life of Jesus may be made visible in our mortal flesh.

So death is at work in us, but life in you.

II Corinthians 4:1-12, var.

We put down our anchor in these words. They were deep enough to hold our calling while we edged our way forward into the unknown future. We began a custom of beginning each workshop by reading those verses with fervor. In different ways, the three of us had laid our lives on the line for this ministry that we had been given "by God's mercy" and thus had no cause to "lose heart." We had not pursued it actively; we had just been open when people asked for our help.

God's mercy was necessary because of the special dangers of deception. Our place in the work required that we "renounce the hidden things of dishonesty." We needed to resist the temptation to live out of a false self by seeming to be more pious than we are, carrying the illusion of having "arrived" spiritually, when underneath we have to wrestle with the same mixture of motives and self-seeking behaviors as everyone else. Life/Work Direction would be about an "open statement of the truth." Our true self, writes Thomas Merton, is simply "the person we are meant to be,"[11] the self bearing God's image and formed by God in our mother's womb.

We are not to "proclaim ourselves" but "Jesus Christ as Lord," and "ourselves your slaves." From the beginning we were equals with the participants, seeking the "light of the knowledge of the glory of God in the face of Jesus Christ." This majestic God of glory was not only the invisible force behind the universe, but an intimate God known in the person of Jesus Christ who walked this earth as a human like ourselves.

Placing this "treasure in clay jars" of our own humanity would make sure that we knew that "the power belongs to God, and does not come from us." We were to live transparent lives so that "the life of Jesus may be seen in us." Any claim on our part that "we know," that we have answers, has to die—"death is at work in us"—in order for new life to be at work in those we served—not as a one-time experience in coming to Christ, but a continuous dying to self in order to live to God.

This is strong language, and conveyed a message that resonated with participants. They also saw their Christian faith as involving a total conversion of life—not being conformed to the culture, but transformed "by the renewing of the mind" as Romans 12:2 puts it. This meant seeing conversion in a new way, not as a one-time event as many Protestants were taught, but a lifelong process of transformation, bringing mind, heart and will into alignment with God—in a word, radically changing us.[12]

Life/Work Direction's part in this process is threefold: affecting thinking, feeling and action:
- We open people up to new ways of thinking that challenge and sometimes reverse their idea of who God is and what faith means. They discover the mystery of God's love and life within them, and find that faith is in a Person rather than in a set of truths. We help them become more comfortable with "not knowing" and yet trusting.
- We encourage people to explore their own hearts, their inner lives, unearthing core gifts as well as obscured motives and feelings, and invite them to fully receive God's love, mercy and forgiveness—the discovery of God's total acceptance of their true selves as they are.
- We listen as they begin to discern their own calling in the world to action, willingly following Jesus—not so much by doing some great thing in the world, but by being who they are, transformed by grace. To experience this level of conversion—transformation of mind, heart, and will—requires wholehearted engagement on our part as

guides. Nothing less will do. As Richard Rohr writes, "it is only transformed people who have the power to transform others, as if by osmosis. This is the way the soul works."[13] In the end, transformation is not our work; it is God's. At Life/Work Direction, we had simply chosen work as the presenting issue and a way of getting to this deeper understanding of Christian conversion.

As might be expected, people came to us focused on work but quickly learned much more was involved. Splashed across the front of our current brochure are the words "Coming Apart," words that can be taken in more than one sense. From the beginning, we looked positively on times when a person was out of work, or dissatisfied, because to us it appeared to be a God-given opportunity to take stock of one's life at a broader and deeper level. This instantly slowed people down, and helped them "come apart and rest" in their rush to find the way forward, maybe even reverse direction in some cases. They often came in agitated, anxious, and eager for immediate answers. Unemployment does that to people. We often pointed to the paradoxical motto on the wall, "We must go slowly; there is not much time." Very quickly, participants adapted to our pace. They felt secure in having a place to come with their worries and fears. They were held, accompanied. This was our way of shifting their attention away from immediate worries about money and job to the issues of calling and the larger meaning of their existence on earth.

Our first priority was on calling to discipleship, and second to work in the world. We took the example of the first disciples who, hearing Jesus' invitation, "Follow me," interpreted this to mean that they should leave their nets (i.e., their career), implying that we do not always follow the expected paths laid out by inheritance or culture in the service of the kingdom. We saw how Jesus modeled intentional "downward mobility"— "humbling himself" in the words from Scripture:

> *Christ Jesus, who, though he was in the form of God, did not regard equality with God as something to be exploited, but emptied himself, taking the form of a slave, being born in human likeness. And being found in human form, he humbled himself and became obedient to the point of death—even death on a cross.*
>
> Philippians 2:6-8

This was not the typical career counseling being offered by professional downtown firms. We did not assume an unbroken spiral of "career advancement." This meant that some persons who completed the workshop made conscious decisions to work less (in jobs for pay) in order to do their "real" work—both the spiritual development of their interior lives and serving others meaningfully in the parish and in the "marketplace." We were advocating a way of thinking about vocation that is not particularly easy to follow because it runs against the grain of the culture that often measures success in terms of money and prestige.

A participant in one of our early workshops, Mark Morrison, illustrates this tension between discipleship and career.

> At the time I was participating in Life/Work, I was struggling with the morality of my occupation as an engineer for a company in the defense industry. The group at Life/Work was great in helping me to know myself better and to process the feelings and turmoil going on inside of me. This helped me to decide that, for me personally, I could no longer work for a company in the defense industry.
>
> This, however, was only half the battle. Now that I had decided to leave my job, I had the problem of deciding what to do. After some more struggling and searching, God opened the door to being hired as an advocate for homeless and low-income people at the Good Shepherd Center in Lawrence, part of Lazarus House Ministries.
>
> Though the pay is considerably less, my job satisfaction has greatly increased. I feel blessed by the simplicity and openness of the people I experience each day. I feel the presence of Christ in these people and this gives me great joy. Though there are many difficult days and disappointments, to be sure, so too there is hope. It is the hope I see and the joy I feel that confirm in me that the decision I made was for the best.
>
> It is the many friends and people in our lives, especially those I found at Life/Work Direction that gave my wife and me the courage to make the decisions. They helped us reach for the dreams that God placed in our hearts.

Life/Work Direction's core vision of discipleship was simple yet broad enough to allow fluidity in the way we worked it out in practice. We were free to experiment with the program, reverse or revise as necessary, so long as the deepest purposes remained at the center like a gyroscope influencing every twist and turn of the design.

PUTTING DOWN ROOTS: THE PEOPLE
Dick Faxon, Don and I were determined not to be encumbered by the usual professional leader-and-group model with its asymmetric distribution of power. We were not the experts, solving problems for those who came; rather we were called to walk with others as they explored their callings. By offering diverse perspectives, we would leave participants freer to make their own judgments. Working in the circle created by a round table accentuated our egalitarian attitude.

The team approach helped each of us make a unique contribution and balance one another's gifts. One participant said, "I was able to see three distinct personalities grapple with my life and ideas. Their responses were equally distinct and vivid." Another affirmed us by saying, "I found three people listening to God." We could ask for nothing greater.

In many ways, the three of us were an unlikely trio. Dick's nature was more reserved and quiet, waiting for the right moment to enter the conversation with laser-like insight and authority. He was a tender man, always courteous, and genuinely interested in the participants. Raised in a home where religion was assumed but expressed formally, he hungered to feel his faith at a heart level. His personal spiritual life was saturated with prayer.

Many participants approached Dick for his healing ministry of prayer. He marked a conference on healing that he attended in the 1970s as a watershed in his life, where he experienced a spiritual awakening so powerful he later termed it a conversion. In recounting his experience from the pulpit in his parish the following week, he could not describe it in words and instead offered to sing a song he had learned at the conference. Standing tall and erect in the pulpit, Dick sang a simple song. He had always longed to be free — to rise above his shyness and inhibitions. That day he did, the result of the power of his encounter with God, the Holy Spirit. Some who followed Dick to Many Mansions were people from his parish who had been deeply affected by Dick's openness and embrace of a connection with God that had ignited "fire in his belly."

I sometimes sensed that it was not easy for Dick to be the third member of a triad that included a married couple — most particularly the two of us. Yet Dick was unflagging in his support of Don and me in our gifts. He could match Don's acuity of perception in the realm of arts and ideas, and they carried on a running conversation from day to day on an abstract level that stimulated them both. Don loved the way Dick brought the outside world into the workplace daily. He would whip out his copy of the *New York Times,* and set it down on the table, pointing to an article he wanted us to read. He stayed abreast of the times — whether in the area of politics, theatre, the arts, or literature — and was a trenchant critic. His critiques often came with a sardonic edge; he loved irony and used it with force.

He was supportive of my nascent interest in contemplative spirituality and tutored me by example. He went on periodic silent retreats himself and encouraged me in this new approach to spiritual practice. Dick's resilience in working with us on staff was astonishing, and it was humbly received for we perceived him to be a big man in heart and in soul.

Don served as counterpoint to both Dick and me with his love of the outrageous, his total immediacy of presence, his enthusiastic hugs, and his spontaneous reactions to the ridiculous. He would not be fenced in by structures or the linearity of curricular plans; he sensed the tempo, gravitated to the beat of the ongoing conversation, introduced the absurd and unexpected. He relied on Dick and me to rein him in if he got too far afield. He greeted participants at the door with open arms exuding warmth and love. They quickly learned that he would speak the truth unequivocally to them from that place of warmth.

The friendship sustained by these two men was a mark of their largeness of heart. On the surface, they presented a contrast: Dick—diffident, always appropriate; and Don—utterly spontaneous and brash. Underneath, they were both men who loved truth. Don spoke it openly, some would say harshly. Dick listened, reflected, and responded. Both were at home with humor. Neither of them would desert the other in a moment of pique over a misunderstanding; loyalty superseded ego.

I valued their relationship with each other and my own with each of them. So there I was—the sole woman—with these two giants; Dick was six foot four, Don six foot two and ample in girth. I held my own because these two men both acknowledged that the work was impossible without me. I was the educator of the group, designing the curriculum and presenting the process to new participants in a way that made sense and drew them in. I wrote the materials, kept track of people and money, and did lots of the practical tasks that kept the ship afloat.

We realized that a vibrant work was already going on in those initial spontaneous workshops at Many Mansions. Our challenge now was to give it a concrete form. This did not mean coming up with a succession of brilliant program ideas. It meant spending endless hours in passionate discussion about the philosophy by which we operated.

I was the one of the three of us who drew diagrams, suggested paradigms that put our ideas into a context or structure, and took copious notes during every conversation. Don posed the probing and provocative questions that helped us think through what we were doing and why. It was a productive, happy time. All of us had the capacity to stand back and observe what we were doing and to articulate that concretely in harmony with our philosophy and principles.

We spent some time considering our relationship to the Church, an issue of particular relevance to Dick who had been steeped in his role as a priest. He asked us, "What distinguishes Life/Work Direction from a church or parish?" We had to consider the extent to which we would continue certain practices Dick had maintained at Many Mansions—reading the lection for the day, conducting a liturgy each noon. Dick wanted to continue certain priestly functions. He imagined taking the sacrament to the sick in nearby hospitals, for example. At the same time, all three of us were firmly committed to an ecumenical stance. Participants often had a dissonant or broken relationship with their local church. One participant told us, "Life/Work provides something that is missing in the church." We adopted the principle of being a separate body from the Church; we were beside it.

"At Life/Work Direction," Dick wrote, "we are seeking those who are missed by the parish priest or are unchurched. This includes those who seek a spiritual base akin to the Desert Fathers, downwardly mobile, solitary, and in touch with the Spirit."

Instead of an institutional connection, Dick was suggesting a more primitive model. The tradition of the Desert Fathers struck a chord in me—the call to come apart in silence in order to listen to an inner voice directing me and transforming daily life by a sense of Christ's presence. It was an approach equally applicable to modern urban life and the ancient deserts of Sinai.

At one point we convened a group of pastors from several denominations to ask them what sort of relationship to churches made sense for them and for us. We did not want to be in competition with the church in any way. We wondered if the pastors would want us to offer workshops within their congregations. To our surprise and I think some relief, they said "No." They recognized what we instinctively knew, that people were far freer to explore the whole range of their belief and disbelief outside of the home parish. They preferred us to offer our program apart from their institutions.

It may also be that they were wary of our rhetoric about discipleship and downward mobility. We might have seemed slightly ungrounded to them. A subtle clue for me resides in a story a reporter from the *Boston Church Life* publication wrote about our efforts.[14] He described our program elements, then said, "Beyond these structures, the most curious aspect about Life/Work Direction is that it seemingly has no structure. They have no model from a book or anywhere else."

Then he quoted me as saying, "We aren't institutionalizing something," and Dick adding, "It depends on us. It depends on Christ. Christ can't be institutionalized. There is a theological reason from my point of view. There is always some discontinuity between the Kingdom and us.

We are dependent on the Spirit. We don't know how the Lord will lead us in the future."

I am then quoted as admitting, "The noninstitutional attitude can be misunderstood. It can't be an evasion of responsibility. It is related to the fact that we don't know."

Our basic structure was absurdly simple. We copied the Many Mansions Articles of Incorporation and by-laws for the most part, taking care to include phrases that would allow us to own property in case we ever needed it. We listed our own three names as the Board of Directors—the minimum required by law. We wanted to be free to move in accordance with our philosophy.

We also wanted to be accountable spiritually and decided on an affiliation with an order of Episcopal monks at the Society of St. John the Evangelist in Cambridge.[15] We arranged to receive spiritual direction together each month from one of the monks. Dick said, "This will keep us in touch with the desert ground of our mission work in the city without losing hope."

PUTTING DOWN ROOTS: THE PARTICIPANTS
Our roots in Many Mansions gave us a gift of inestimable value: a critical mass of young persons ripe for the process we were offering. These loving, energetic, winsome, wacky, eager, prayerful people became the first participants in the workshops that became Life/Work Direction. Because of the ecumenical nature of the Many Mansions project, we had instant contacts in a wide range of Christian traditions dispersed over greater Boston. As participants completed a workshop, they told their friends who in turn told their friends, creating a continuous loop. This kept a steady stream of people coming through our doors. Life/Work Direction would never have to advertise.

Originally, the people at Many Mansions had been attracted to the promise that venture held for them. They liked moving beyond the confines of their own parishes to a group of people alive with contagious spiritual energy. Some were unemployed; others uncertain about their career prospects, and all were looking for a way to make a meaningful connection between life and work. They sensed a refreshing spirit of joy and hopefulness in the possibility of finding a more integrated life.

They told us that they found people at Life/Work Direction who talked about the spiritual life freely, who thought that a calling began with a desire to follow Jesus and whose consciences were awakened to the needs of the poor. It probably also helped that we were not a church, making the hard questions and doubts fair game.

PUTTING DOWN ROOTS: THE PROGRAM

The core vision, the people we were, and the participants we attracted, comprised the basis for the program we developed. What underlay our thinking was the classic tension between action—the desire for *doing*, and contemplation—the surrender to *being*. In Biblical terms, it is the story of Mary and Martha in Luke 10. Martha was busy "about much serving" while Mary "sat at Jesus' feet" listening. We cannot take sides here; Mary and Martha are not to be separated. Contemplation leads to right action. Being with Jesus, listening and reflecting and feeling his heartbeat, leads us to respond to others in the world with both love and wisdom.

To use the imagery of water, contemplation without an outlet in action becomes a stagnant pool. Action without contemplation turns us into compulsive helpers who are cut off from the freshly flowing stream of life that feeds us.

We were not inclined to rush into devising a curriculum full of career assessment techniques. We knew we needed to slow down the action at the very beginning. We did not expect to turn people into contemplatives, but we needed to begin in a way that would help them become observers of their lives and inner processes before they were ready to choose work that expressed and even amplified who they were, or led them in a helpful new direction. We used storytelling to elicit this sort of reflection: the life story, their spiritual journey, remembrances of fulfilling experiences, their history of relationships, their attitudes toward money. These laid the foundation for the exploration of their gifts and aptitudes for a place in the world of work that was consonant with their true being.

In weaving Life/Work Direction's tapestry, it is those critical vertical warp threads of life and work, however you name them—contemplation and action, being and doing, who you *are* as related to what you *do*—that determine the overall structure. Those threads can be detected in the first workshops we offered, and have stood the tests of time since. We elaborated on those primary themes of *being* and *doing* year by year in the way we constructed the curriculum. Because those threads are so basic, they lend themselves to variations in color and fiber in the weft strands that intersect them. The elemental structure does not need to be replaced.

THE PRACTICAL MATTERS OF MONEY AND SPACE

Money
We had to address the issue of financial support. We would depend on God for financial resources; money would not determine the direction of the ministry. The fees charged for workshops ($5 per evening for each person for twelve sessions) were not sufficient to support the basic expenses of rent, supplies, and staff. We held outside jobs and took no money from Life/Work Direction when we began. I was teaching courses in Self Assessment and Career Development at Northeastern University. Don kept his job at the Chinese bookstore followed by a series of doorman positions on Beacon Hill and in Back Bay. Dick knew that he would be able to support himself from his family real estate business and his wife's income as a professor of Art History at Simmons College. He also consistently sought part-time priestly roles and maintained his association with the diocese in his typical loyal, but detached, manner. He was in the diocesan world, but not exactly of it. He was drawn to the margins.

One of the first written documents in our files is a mimeographed sheet entitled "Philosophy of Money." We did not think in terms of a "budget plan," but a philosophy. We articulated four basic principles:

1. Dependence on God.
   We acknowledge dependence on God for our financial needs.
2. The Principle of Self-Support.
   We will work to support ourselves through part-time work outside until there is sufficient money coming in to justify drawing salaries. We recognize the value of staff persons keeping in touch with the persons they serve.
3. Working and Living Simply.
   As staff members, we will keep salaries at modest levels and operating expenses at a minimum.
4. Seeking Support from the Community of Participants.
   We will seek financial support primarily from persons who know our work from firsthand contact and therefore have a basis for believing in it.

We were averse to fundraising on a grand scale. Don and I had not had to do that at the Urban Life Center, and Dick was reluctant to appeal to Many Mansions' donors for more funds. We decided to follow point four of our philosophy and look to the embryonic community of recent participants for help. We would call them members, and ask them to pray for us and contribute regularly—a suggested donation was $10 a month. We wanted to maintain a three-dimensional relationship and not just pocket their checks. We began referring to them as *membranes* to indicate they constituted our permeable borders keeping us in touch with the world. We gave them hand-painted membership cards in a special ceremony. We scheduled an evening of "storytelling" to cement their feeling of community with one another and with us. We wrote them newsletters, crudely typed with handwritten titles, sharing stories about participants. We took members into our confidence, described our plans, and asked for feedback.

The results were revealing. The community feeling was there, warm and reassuring, but it could not be based on financial giving for many of the members had limited means. We were not tempted to rely on members' contributions for our expenses. The amounts trickling in were given out of love for us, the "widow's mite" spoken of in the gospels.

We added another surprising dimension: tithing excess income! We told members that every six months, we would take 10% of any income received over budget and give it to a ministry serving needy persons in Boston, the United States, or overseas. Their gifts and fees were not only used to defray Life/Work's immediate and basic expenses; we wanted to embrace ministries beyond the perimeters of Life/Work Direction in our concerns, especially those who were serving the poor in ways we could not. These included Third World projects of the Jubilee Fund, housing rehabilitation for the poor overseen by Christians for Urban Justice, and Sojourner House in Roxbury providing housing for displaced families. This practice continued for the first eight years.

Throughout, a spiritually oriented relationship to money was deemed essential. We didn't want financial concerns to rule. We knew that dependency on wealthy donors could shortcut the spiritual energy. Perhaps it was our work ethic that determined our insistence on "paying as we go," protecting us from overstepping our resources or relying on entities that were unsympathetic to our basic goals and way of working. We saw that the amount of money—or lack of it—provided reasonable limits, generated creative solutions, and encouraged the right kind of dependence on God, on others, and on ourselves.

The corresponding temptation for us was subtler: pride in our independence and a lack of the humility required in asking for support. Perhaps we felt that our humility had been sufficiently exercised by our move to Dorchester. We were determined from the beginning not to have to advertise or promote. We trusted that by relying on referrals the quality of the work would determine its continuance. We reasoned that if Life/Work Direction was a good idea and met needs it would grow, and if it failed in these it would be better to let it languish and die. We were not heavily invested in preserving an organization over time but rather in being fruitful in the work we were engaged in at the present.

Space

The space at 107 Savin Hill Avenue seemed adequate in the summer and fall months of 1981. Then cold weather came, and we began encountering the uncertainties of a sputtering furnace in our new location. As the winter winds whipped over the storefronts on the avenue, we huddled inside, wrapping layers of sweaters and coats around us. Not to be confounded, we called a crew of participants together to solve the problem using materials at hand. Attempting to add ingenuity to our decorative style, funky as it was, we applied multiple layers of newspaper on the walls and then tacked colorful quilts and blankets on top to block out the cold air. We still shivered.

And yet the stream of workshop participants continued, week after week, coming by word of mouth from former participants. We were tapping into a hardy cohort of persons, most in their late twenties, some of whom had come to Boston expressly to engage in some form of Christian ministry.

Down the block, Harry the Barber recognized our plight with the malfunctioning furnace. "Psst," he said to us one cold day in the winter of 1982, "Talk to the landlord of my building. I think the tenants next door are vacating." We looked at the tiny space next to his barbershop, and wondered how we could fit all our ponderous files, desks and chairs into this minuscule space. But the price was right, and included heat from a furnace that worked.

A carpenter friend, Dan Calcaterra, ingeniously helped us create the right kind of space with partitions. Though only a nook-and-cranny, the workshop room was just big enough for our round table and 8-10 chairs, bookcases and a cluster of plants at the grill-protected window. We carved out a "convenience" kitchen boasting sink, hot plate, refrigerator, and makeshift pantry shelves; and a slender office space with a comfy corner for one-on-one counseling, despite no outside ventilation or light. The following spring, we finally announced our location to the world with a bold sign, "Life/Work Direction," above the storefront window, hand-painted by Gary Weiland, one of our participants.

Finally, we were at the end of our "space trip," at least for the present. The fifth floor at 25 West Street downtown had been too big, the storefront at 107 Savin Hill Avenue, too cold and costly. Our third location at 101 Savin Hill Avenue was Goldilocks' "just right." The three bears settled in for a long stay.

Still, we had to reckon with the reality that we were in Dorchester. St. Williams School stood across the street, with its daily afternoon effluvium of uniformed kids spilling onto the street. Pre-teenagers began noticing our little hole-in-the-wall operation, and found it unfamiliar and odd. The kids began engaging in a combination of creative and annoying acts of minor harassment. We would be in session with a group when suddenly we were startled by a loud THWACK on our door—usually at the moment of a particularly intense pause for reflection.

The little Vietnamese Saigon Market that popped up on the corner and provided a colorful array of food also became a target of harassment. We got drawn into the fray, perhaps more rambunctiously than was wise. The fracas subsided, but after several weeks of relative quiet the boys returned with smoke bombs, one thrown at the Vietnamese store and another through our mail slot. Imagine our consternation when we discovered that one of the more inventive kids had figured out how to lock us inside by inserting a small stick into the ring meant to hold our padlock, essentially making it impossible for us to exit. There we were, three giant adults helplessly stuck inside our work place. The kids were delighted with their triumph. It took a phone call to summon rescue.

All this stirred up our own creative retaliatory juices. We considered adding another door, replacing this one with a steel door, changing the interior walls and putting the workshop space in the back, moving elsewhere in Boston, or strangling the kids. In the end, we decided we needed to pray for our small-sized tormentors. Remarkably, the kids soon tired of the game and the thumping decreased except for occasional snowballs thrown against our door in the winter.

The Saigon Market did not fare as well. Someone backed a pickup truck into their front door one day, demolishing part of the interior. The Vietnamese proprietors packed up and left for a less hostile environment half a mile away.

A couple of pastors of a nearby church moved into the Market's space. We were between two worlds, growing accustomed to music and voices on both sides of us—Harry's barbershop full of men joking and talking on one side and the church fellowship people singing and conversing on the other. We hunkered down in between and set about our work with contentment and optimism.

I always chronicled our progress during these years, writing in a log for our archives. During this period of our life, I wrote these words in an attempt to convey some of the sense of what we thought we were about in this strange enterprise on a side street in Dorchester:

Somehow, what I'm trying to say through all of this is that Life/Work Direction is attempting to blaze a trail, as it were, where no clear roadway lies. We mean to follow Jesus—and if that entails leaving our nets, or taking the lowest place, or girding ourselves with a towel, or speaking the truth to the culture when this is difficult, we want to be ready. As I write this, it sounds noble and idealistic. We don't want this to be rhetoric. We are seeking to carry out this desire (to follow Jesus) in our own lives literally.

It's quiet here in the workshop room, save for the scratching of this pen, the buzz of the crippled clock in the corner, an occasional sigh from Don pondering his poetry, and the hum of a car or two passing by on Savin Hill Avenue. Dick went home early to nurse a cold that is coming on. In a couple of hours, the evening workshop participants will arrive, and so we listen for the voice of Jesus in the stillness—preparing to hear Him in others as they begin "life stories" tonight.

I was aware, even then, that I was writing Life/Work Direction's story.

CHAPTER 8

Creating Community:
seeing a pattern emerge

1981-1990

THE SPIRIT OF COMMUNITY RUNS LIKE A BRIGHT THREAD through the first few years. Meeting as a group was central to our beginnings, and our curriculum was adapted to making the most of group interaction. Eating supper together began the process of knitting people into community. Sharing one another's life stories in the workshop deepened connections. People in one workshop referred their friends, thus creating a connection between people from different groups.

It is hard to define exactly what it was that drew people to the little storefront to be part of the vocational process. One person typical of those who came to meet with us was Carmel Franciscovich (now Cuyler). "Life/Work Direction is where I came home to myself spiritually," she told me.

I came to faith in the middle of my college years. It was an experiential and intuitive thing. Once I met Jesus, that was a constant. I picked up things from different places. I grew up spiritually at Park Street Church, where I was nurtured intellectually in the Bible and the fundamentals of the faith. It gave my faith form, and did not contradict my more intuitive experience.

One day in 1983, I was sitting on a park bench on the Boston Common talking with Phil Mangano. I told him I had decided to leave my job in public relations. Phil had been in a Life/Work Direction workshop and he saw I was the sort of person who would appreciate their approach. "You need to meet these people," he said.

> *So I called, and came down for a workshop. At Life/Work Direction, I knew Jesus in the same way that was presented there. It was seamless with my experience. They were living out of faith organically. I understood their being in Dorchester, surrounded by the working poor. It felt vulnerable and down-to-earth.*

From the time Carmel came through our doors, there was a mutual feeling of kindred spirits in the way we experienced our faith. After she participated in the basic workshop, we asked her to assist us in two subsequent workshops, having detected her valuable qualities of leadership. Carmel joined other groups we offered as well. And when we convened informal advisory groups, she was first on our list to invite because we valued her input. Eventually, she joined our board and stayed for twelve years. To this day, she remains connected to us in an advisory capacity.

A self-selecting community was arising among persons who held certain spiritual sensibilities in common. We as staff did not stand apart from the community that began to grow around Life/Work Direction, for we were an integral part of it. A feeling of camaraderie developed as we wanted and needed others' help. We convened a handful of participants to discuss our ideas and give us advice and suggestions for future plans. Although the basic workshop continued to be a centerpiece of Life/Work Direction's ministry and the point of entry for most folks, these advisors began asking for more follow through afterward. One of them wondered aloud, "What do you do with the life that emerged within the process of the workshop, especially when you reach a turning point?" She felt the need for community "to support that emerging life."

Another person said he was "learning to be away from Life/Work," i.e., struggling in the workplace to apply what he had learned, and he needed some help. Others felt similarly:
- *I have a hard time dealing with the lack of affinity with others when I am not with the Life/Work people.*
- *What I find here is a like-minded/heartedness. It is hard to say where I want to go. I am still figuring out where I am!*
- *Rather than developing a common ministry together, I see us supporting each other's vocation.*
- *I'm weighing right now whether my ministry at my church may be a vocation. The support and interaction at Life/Work has been nourishing to me in a dimension I do not get anywhere else. It enables me to do a better job.*

Some struggled to express a unique aspect at Life/Work Direction that suggested an attitude of openness and a willingness to "not know" answers.
- *Life/Work allows you to "be in the middle" and to not know, to have things suspended. I wouldn't have had the courage to do this without the group. I could listen to that "quiet voice" within me.*
- *There was something at Life/Work—people talking about God—which I couldn't find anywhere else. I needed to know others who were making a real commitment to Jesus.*
- *I want to live with the kinds of people I found here where I feel I am on the edge of hearing God's voice. I am grateful to Life/Work and its people. I feel a tenderness.*

One person talked about a kind of "madness" she felt in herself, as a person striving to live counter to the culture—a holy insanity that she felt was understood by others here.
- *Life/Work's mission is to people who feel that madness. I can go through an unstructured stage in my life because of my trust in the word of Christ to me, and the presence of the other "mad" persons.*

Through these conversations, we came to appreciate the hunger for a deeper level of community that brought people to our door. The following year, we convened another advisory group of participants to talk about the work. The pressure for more contact beyond the basic workshop was mounting. As the advisors talked, it was clear that they were hungering for more of what they had begun receiving and urged us to offer something beyond the basic workshop:
- *The workshop is crucial, but people need to go farther.*
- *The workshop takes you only part way. Some things are left hanging.*
- *It is a mistake to just do the basic workshop. Maybe shift the bulk of your time from workshop process to follow through with people.*

One person suggested that offering a second workshop would allow people from different workshops to meet each other. Another thought that a second workshop would "get down to business spiritually by sharing spiritual histories," an idea that became an integral part of our curriculum from that point on.

So we did what they asked. We reduced the number of basic workshops offered to allow space to insert advanced workshops. We weren't sure what form these might take, but we knew we could rely on the participants themselves to help us shape the content.

This resulted in the creation of "Bethany Groups"—a name we took from the story of the Bethany home of Martha and Mary and Lazarus, symbolic of a place where Jesus found community. The first Bethany group was experimental, and persons with a commitment to the ministry of Life/Work shaped the design and content. We set a general agenda, then crafted questions and exercises that would elicit responses to the issues people raised. We used stories, images, and metaphors. We worked in pairs. We said, "Ask each other good questions."

It was through Bethany Groups that Scott Walker once again appeared on Life/Work Direction's doorstep eager to participate and as it turned out, to use his special skill as an educator in its deepest meaning— "one who educes, draws out from others."

He recalls his experience:

In Scott's words

What was wonderful about the Bethany group was the invitation to experiment with different ways of learning with a group of people. On the occasion that I was responsible for leading the group, I was stimulated by the stories of the healing of the blind in the Gospels. I wondered what the change must have been like—to move from a darkened world to one of light. I was curious about the blind person's heightened awareness of his surroundings, and what it was like to anticipate Jesus' actions and feel his presence in other ways as he engaged them. Did blindness sometimes serve as a gift to open the eyes of the heart, and how significant could it be to develop a heart that can see in the dark before the light arrives?

With these questions in mind, I began by asking everyone to close their eyes. We sat in silence for a few minutes, allowing a different kind of environmental awareness to rise. The sounds of cars and pedestrian conversations passing outside the storefront door contributed to the sense of being in the middle of activity yet strangely separate from it. I then read the story of the healing of the blind man in the ninth chapter of the Gospel of John, the one where the man gains his sight only after his encounter with Jesus, and where the local religious authorities who claim to know the truth immediately question the validity of his experience.

While we sat in the dark, I read the story in sections punctuated by sounds associated with the work of God in creation. I poured out a pitcher of water into a bucket and splashed my hands in it. At another point I slowly struck a match across a matchbox to light a candle. Both were sounds rich with associations. Once the story had been fully read, I asked the group to open their eyes and talk about their different experiences. What does it mean to be given real sight and how does this relate to the experience of waiting in faith?

The threads connecting Life/Work Direction and Scott were growing stronger. We detected his gift in creative group leadership; his use of symbol and experiential devices to amplify his presentation of Biblical story and elicit new ways of perceiving pointed forward to his future calling. Shortly after this, Scott asked if we would convene a new group focused specifically on Group Dynamics. He wanted to test his leadership ability with peers and learn all he could from us as he continued in his role leading interns at CUJ. None of us foresaw how his gifts might come to be part of Life/Work Direction, but the way was being prepared.

Another thread woven into the fabric early on involved Stephanie Smith (now Choo), one of several persons like Scott who had moved to inner-city Boston after college. She participated in a workshop at Life/Work Direction and then returned to take part in a number of other groups that emerged.

Stephanie had grown up in a household that did not emphasize personal faith, but during her college years at Princeton she came across C. S. Lewis' *Mere Christianity*. Lewis' writing made her want to know more about Jesus. She joined a campus Bible study and began reading *Sojourners* magazine, which influenced her thinking about Jesus' attitude toward the poor. After graduation, she moved to Dorchester and joined the residential community of Christians for Urban Justice, where Joe Verla was also a member and Scott led the summer internship program.

Once in Boston, she first visited Park Street Church and later slipped a few doors up the street to the Paulist Center where she found spiritual nourishment in the liturgy and the socially engaged culture of an unusual Roman Catholic congregation. She had been reading books by Thomas Merton, a Trappist monk who wrote extensively about contemplative prayer and meditation, and Dorothy Day of the Catholic Worker Movement. She found this combination of contemplation and action both compelling and challenging. She tells her story:

In the fall of 1981, I came to a Life/Work Direction workshop. I had learned of this new organization from people I knew well — Scott Walker and

Joe Verla—and had a sense that what was happening there could support both the inner and outer explorations in which I was engaged. I received pastoral counseling at the Danielsen Center at Boston University, and was seeing that my childhood in an affluent family and community had emphasized experiencing life "from the outside in," measuring myself and others by outward success and appearances. I longed to experience my life "from the inside out," to know God at my center, to learn more about my God-given gifts and abilities, and to live them out in the world.

Life/Work Direction turned out to be exactly the right place for me at that time. Little did I know that for many years thereafter it would continue to be a place of deep sustenance and support, and an important part of my own life work.

Her interest and continuing participation were weaving Stephanie into the fabric of what we were creating at Life/Work Direction. None of us anticipated how many times these threads would intersect in the next two decades.

EXPANDING COMMUNITY THROUGH GROUPS
Soon we began spawning groups to meet diverse needs: one for men, another for women, an arts group, a spiritual direction group, and an Enneagram study group. We experimented with an Issues Forum to "deal with issues that arose out of the tension of living out the kingdom of God in the world, discerning what Jesus is saying about each issue." These groups were one more way to respond to the expressed desire to stay in touch with us and with each other.

My interest in therapy precipitated my introduction of a group for several women who were currently in therapy, based on Eugene Gendlin's book, *Focusing*.[16] I asked Stephanie Smith to lead it with me, as I recognized her affinity for psychological approaches. Like me, she had found Gendlin's focusing process to be both instinctive and useful in deriving tangible benefit from her own therapy.

My reading of Catherine de Hueck Doherty's *Poustinia*[17] prompted my interest in an exploration of contemplatively oriented reflection and study. The word "Poustinia" refers to a place of solitude where we find the God who dwells within us. It can be a hut in the desert, a house in the city, a room or closet in our own homes, or it can be within us—in the heart, or—like Mary—in the womb where each of us is pregnant with Christ. A "poustinik" is a listening person, whose listening is deep—a person who rises from prayer and silence to be available to others in need.

We began a series of Poustinia groups where our purpose was to meet

God in silence together and grow in imagination and insight in the way we heard the Word of God so that we would experience Christ speaking to us directly and through the Word. That meant including some close reading of a Gospel narrative with guided meditation, cloaked in silence before, during and after. We included sharing at the end of the time. We made a point of not including refreshments, in order to retain the intentionality and form that best supports this kind of experience. Poustinia became a lasting symbol of work I later explicitly named Spiritual Companionship, a direction toward which I was slowly being led in my own life, as well as in my work.

※

The proliferation of all these groups was both an expression of community and a force that intensified it. It became natural to get together in social contexts as well, such as annual Labor Day picnics called "bashes." One especially memorable gathering took place in 1986 in Jamaica Plain at the home of Paula and Dan Calcaterra. It seems that they wanted to move a tool shed in their back yard to a spot 150 feet away. We assured them that this could be accomplished at our Labor Day bash by assembling enough people with strong muscles and the accompanying spirit of camaraderie that marked our get-togethers. It was a stretch, especially for a couple of the senior citizens who volunteered. After a picnic supper, we corralled the strongest persons present. On the count of three, they inched the burden across the yard while sweating profusely, and with one mighty lurch, they dropped the shed in place, an unforgettable feat.

At other times members gathered together for an evening of storytelling and a backyard picnic. At a party in a church basement, we centered our activity on the "Party Game," a device we used in our vocational process. Dividing people according to their identified work orientations (Artistic, Social, Enterprising, etc.) generated interaction between members of different workshop groups around common aptitudes.

There were a few retreats as well. The first year, a small group of us went to Brian Murdoch's family cottage on the Maine/New Hampshire border. A few years later, I took a Women's Group on a weekend retreat. Another retreat took place in the mid 1990s with a prominent role taken by Scott Walker in its preparation. Over the years, we sometimes imagined a next step for our work might involve some form of retreat experience. It would be a few years before we would be in a position to incorporate retreats into the fabric of the Life/Work Direction experience, and it would be under Scott's leadership.

Another way of sustaining the spirit of community over the years was the newsletter. We had an instinctive impulse to link participants with one another through written communication. The letters were written in an era before computer graphics and word processing, and featured handcrafted headings and primitive hand-drawn illustrations. The tone was folksy, mentioning participants by name, since so many knew each other from the various groups. We even spread information about job openings when we knew of them. Whatever the form, the content tended to be personal and informal—an expression of the assumption of shared values and goals.

MOVING FROM GROUP WORK TO INDIVIDUAL WORK
The year 1986 marked a basic shift in the work. After the first five years, it became increasingly difficult to put a group together with five persons who had the same night free. Since demand for our services continued unabated, we wondered how we might continue to meet the need of people coming to our doors. Don had been sensing that the group experience tended to dilute the depth to which we were able to go, so was quick to suggest an alternative: that we offer the Life/Work Direction process—which was now formulated as an ordered curriculum—to individuals rather than groups.

If we were weaving a tapestry called Life/Work Direction, we were doing it somewhat blindly from the back without seeing the pattern emerging on the front. A colorful thread—"work with groups"— was being cut, and a new color called "work with individuals" woven in. The cut would turn out to be temporary, but one of long duration, and a major part of the overall design.

Admittedly, there was a loss when we stopped meeting with groups. The input of differing perspectives from peers was gone. "I never realized how differently eight people can view anything!" one participant told us. People loved the interaction with kindred souls. When the focus changed to work with individuals, people lost that sense of camaraderie with others provided by groups.

By contrast, there were unexpected positive effects. The impact of three of us meeting with one person intensified the experience for each participant. People exclaimed about the unparalleled privilege of having the undivided attention of three people for an hour a week over a period of several months. We also realized that there had been times in our group work when some participants were "sitting on" the issues raised and not opening up. We did not know if this was an inevitable result of the psychology of groups, or if it was our lack of expertise in attending to the special needs of group dynamics. For the next two decades we shifted away from group work and focused on individuals.

Along the way, we discovered an ancient symbol that captured our process. It was the "mandorla" as discussed in Robert Johnson's helpful book, *Owning Your Own Shadow*.[18] The symbol consists of two overlapping circles intersected by a cross. The almond-shaped segment is called a mandorla, the Italian word for almond. It can represent any two opposites that present a contradiction—doing and being, light and shadow, the demands of inner life and outer work.

People who appeared on our doorstep often were in a "mandorla" space between two states of being. Sometimes their conflict was between their ideals and values and the way they lived; at other times it was between their self-image and the hidden reality of the true self. A number of participants confessed to a dissatisfaction with the religious experience they had grown up with; they were feeling deeper hungers that seemed to oppose the old religious forms and were looking for a way of reconciling inner contradictions. Often something had broken down which they had relied on in the past, or they were sensing a need for something new and were not clear about what it was. Some were experiencing an impasse in their outer life and work and a staleness had crept into the daily routine. Whatever the case, these were all signals pointing to the need to cultivate the inner wellsprings of the soul so that their life and work in the world might flow from a fresh source. We saw our work with people as a soul journey.

Ancient wisdom tells us that the mandorla space is where God is, symbolized by the cross in the center of the image holding the two circles together. We took the mandorla image for our logo, knowing that we were called to come alongside people who were in the mandorla space of their lives, helping them hold the tension in the present between the unexamined past and unknown future and find ways to integrate these. Our redesigned brochure with its prominent title, "Inner Journeys," marked the intensity of focus in our work with individuals. This precipitated further refinement of the curriculum to support a deeper channel of work with a population that became increasingly diverse in background. Work would continue to be the surface issue, but many people came out of a place of less defined spiritual hunger where life and work had equal valence.

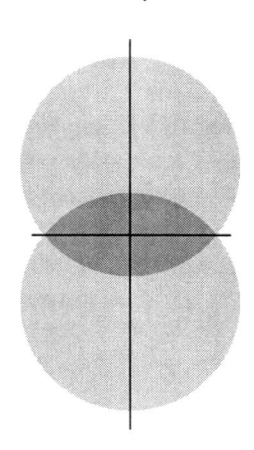

Mandorla

THE PROCESS
We developed a simple curriculum consisting of three modules that were both inclusive and adaptable.

Module 1. Who Are You?
- We hone in on who persons are before attempting to talk about what they do. We begin with hearing their life story—and not as a formal chronology but as a series of vignettes that tease out unexpected memories. We ask, "What did it feel like to be you growing up?"
- This is followed by stories of satisfying experiences outside of work that brought fulfillment. From these stories, we identify "core traits" that predict the kind of work that fits a person's particular gifts. This is one of several points where a participant's creative collation of the material may result in an artistic rendering.
- We then pause lest this exciting discovery of gifts makes a participant rush off to write a resumé based on these findings. We spend time analyzing those gifts in terms of their corresponding hazards—a sober reflection for everyone. Participants are invited to see how some aspects of their ways of functioning in the world work to their detriment, contributing to dissatisfaction in their present job. This is an important break in the forward movement.
- The last piece of this exploration of "who you are" is the tracing of the person's spiritual journey and a creative depiction of their image of God—past and present. Asking for an image defuses any expectation of a set "correct" response. Participants can air their conflicts and doubts safely in this environment. So often, the image creates a powerful opening, saying more than "religious language" can, and points toward what needs attention.

Module 2. What is Important to You?
We next direct the participant's attention to three threads woven into their life experience that influence the final design in their choice of vocation: their relationships; their attitudes toward and experience with money; and their preferred work orientations and environments.
- Many participants discover that the most troubling issue on their minds often has to do with significant relationships in their life.
- Exploring their experience with money in their family of origin and the way they are influenced by the culture's dominant attitudes toward money reveals another factor in the way one's work choices get skewed.
- When we examine work orientations, a participant begins to see how their being fits into doing. We have adapted a few standard tools that

define six different work environments and orientations. This is another point where participants use their creative gifts to come up with an object or drawing that expresses their unique slant on the information that they have discovered. They often come in thrilled by what they have produced to symbolize their orientation to work environments. A light goes on for them and for us because the object they have presented comes totally from within them. We are glad we do not know what people should do with their lives; they are the only ones who can discover it.

Module 3. Why Do You Do What You Do?
- The final module treats motivations, beginning with those that are unconscious. The use of the Enneagram[19] is helpful with many participants, as it charts nine unconscious emotional energies we use to navigate our way in the world. It is a powerful spiritual tool when used correctly, as it points out the characteristic gifts of each type along with the concomitant hazards. When participants are ready to receive this insight, they often speak of it as being the single most important part of the entire process. It is integrating to discover the core dynamic energizing them in the way they interact with others, cope with life's trials, and solve the problems of daily life. The result is clarity of insight and the impetus to open up this core energy to God's grace.
- We elicit a participant's motivations on the conscious level by hearing stories of times when they were highly motivated. Thus, a pattern emerges—and based on all the work done thus far, they return the next time with their version of "A Life Sentence."
- Bringing the process to an end means identifying concrete next steps for them to take and offering them networking contacts to help them on their way. We are not surprised when some participants come back to us for further contact, because we did not conceive of the three-part curriculum as a magic formula leading to a single "final answer." More often than not, the inner work begun within the vocational process creates hunger for an even deeper journey. Through the years, it has become natural for participants to return for further work with us. Some ask for spiritual direction or Listening Prayer, others for couples work, and still others come for support at critical transition points.

The simplicity of the three-module design belies the intricacy of applying this to work with each unique person. We created it to be flexible so that it would fit whether the participant was 28 or 50, sophisticated or simple, a skeptic or grounded in lifelong faith, immature or seasoned emotionally. We became adept in adapting the basic skeletal plan to each person, changing the order of some elements if this seemed wise, asking a person to use more artistic creativity in presenting stories if we sensed this would help. The work was a collaboration involving all of us, continuing an ethos of community, even though we were no longer convening groups. After all, Jesus' definition of community was "where two or three are gathered in my name, I am there among them." (Matthew 18:20) This was ample basis for a community as far as we were concerned.

CHAPTER 9

Looking in the Mirror:
examining the design

L IFE/WORK DIRECTION WAS ENDLESSLY ANALYZED. The three of us held up a mirror to our work daily, subjecting everything we were doing to constant self-scrutiny. We parsed the language we used to describe our philosophy. We stated our goals and principles, then refined what we meant by them. We tried to look at our activities in the light of current trends—in the church, in the culture, in education and the arts and psychological movements. We reveled in metaphors and images, definitely being word people. We kept drawing new pictures to illustrate our work, our relationships to each other, and our connection to other forces in society.

Sifting through my sheaf of notes from those spring months in 1981 when our little enterprise was embryonic and just poking its head out of the rubble as Many Mansions ebbed away, I find a densely typed paper of questions Dick had prepared and brought in for our response. He signed it with a playful flourish as "Richard B. Faxon, Esq." The questions were quintessential Dick, basic and searching; our responses were equally pointed and clear. He used the pronoun "you" indicating he had not yet embraced his role in the ministry. "What kind of organization do you see yourselves becoming—education or counseling? Would your outreach be local, regional, or national? Why locate in Dorchester? How would you support yourselves financially?"

In several respects, his questions were remarkably prescient, anticipating future developments, asking if we anticipated owning a house where we might live and work—something that did not come into being for another ten years. His allusion to what we now call our contemplative approach (his terms were "the monastic" and "silence") was prophetic of an orientation that began to emerge in our early Poustinia groups and later in the practice of spiritual direction.

Although we did a lot of self-evaluation, we knew we needed outside input as well. Three occasions in the early years were significant, each focusing on a particular angle, and using different resources—a monk, an educator/sociologist, and a pastoral psychologist.

1. WHAT DOES OUR CHRISTIAN COMMITMENT MEAN?

Before making the move to Dorchester, we instinctively turned outside our little nest of three for input from one of the monks at the Society of St. John the Evangelist, Robert Rea. He met with a sampling of participants from our first five groups and reported his findings to us during an all-day retreat. That conversation resulted in our clarifying our overtly Christian commitment in the work, meaning that those persons with a more secular orientation who had been drawn to our initial efforts would not be involved in direct leadership.

2. DOES OUR PROCESS WORK IN ACHIEVING ITS GOALS?

By 1983, we decided to do a more extensive evaluation and turned to Ben Mehrling, educator and former minister. Ben was the one who had lured Don and me to Boston in the first place in 1979, offering us an apartment in the triple-decker he had bought. Before he met with us, Ben began the evaluation by asking the three of us on staff to articulate Life/Work Direction's goals and philosophy in writing. After he observed one of our workshops, he interviewed a small group of participants in his home.

Ben saw our work sociologically as a "contemporaneous project" in tune with the times. In his perception, our wholistic approach mirrored aspects of the humanistic psychology movement gaining ascendancy in some quarters. He saw the focus on self-fulfillment in harmony with the ethos of American individualism. The current pressing problem of unemployment in society was linked with changing career expectations of young persons for meaningful work and the corresponding shift in higher education to address those vocational aspirations.

As a sociologist, Ben was wary of the emphasis on American individualism and self-fulfillment to the extent that it neglected systemic approaches to social justice. Our backgrounds held a tension between those approaches as well. Don and I had come from a hard-edged interpretation of societal justice that we promulgated with Christian college students in Chicago. Dick longed for a more visceral connection with people across the dividing lines of race and class. At the same time, all three of us had reasons for highly valuing the self-fulfillment of the individual—my psychological orientation, Don's deep respect for the place and role of the artist as a visionary seer of a culture, and Dick's immersion in ministries of healing. It was not clear to Ben how these tensions would be released into a comprehensive Christian vision equal to the demands of the times.

This evaluation forced us to consider whether or not we were reinforcing an American-style individualism that encourages "getting as much as one can from the system," an attitude of greed in the larger culture that when exaggerated would later contribute to the near collapse of the U.S. economy in 2008. As we mulled over this issue in 1983, we decided that our approach "depoliticized" people and taught them to detach from cultural pressures, and that rather than emphasizing individualism we actually stressed community—a major focus in the early years. As we continued to grow, we found that concerns for social justice and for enrichment of the inner spiritual life could be powerfully integrated.[20]

Ben made sure we got helpful explicit feedback about the impact of our actual workshops. The result was an interesting mix of contradictory statements—some compliments, some complaints, but no consensus. For example, a participant's comment that "the group was not emotional enough" was balanced out by another saying that "it was too emotional." Someone saying "discussions sometimes strayed from the point," offset the complaint that "the exercises were done too hurriedly."

The comments on staff members had the same double quality, revealing how clearly participants assessed our strengths and weaknesses: "Dick is a summarizer, has knowledge and authority. He doesn't talk enough." "Don pursues relentlessly, is imaginative and challenging. He sometimes creates confrontation for its own sake." "Eunice sees new possibilities, a non-parental mother, open, 'the indispensable one,' but sometimes interprets people's experiences for them."

Ben noticed that participants were quick to see attitudinal changes, but slower to identify behavioral changes. The changes in behavior that emerged were typical: "I got directed away from a job change." "I left my job and took two part-time jobs that fit me better." "I worked part-time and could affirm it." In our thinking, the attitudinal change was the more important. We knew behavioral change takes time, and that it cannot easily be measured. In addition, we did not have to know, not having a packaged outcome in mind.

Ben identified our Christian basis as being important to participants for its particular orientation. Not having an organizational affiliation with a church left us a little undefined in others' minds. My lifelong involvement in parachurch organizations made me feel at home with a level of detachment from the church as an institution. Don's secular Jewish background left him free of association with the church. As a clergyman, Dick's feelings were more layered. He was the one, however, to insist on an ecumenical stance that opened us to persons from a variety of religious orientations or with no affiliation at all. This prompted us to present material in language that was accessible to the seeker as well as to those grounded in a similar faith experience. We did not see ourselves as confronting the church or in dialectic with it, but as a servant coming alongside.

Ben saw Life/Work as very dependent on the three of us. He saw that we were consciously not institutionalizing. He warned against ingrownness, suggesting we look to outside resources for our own growth. Since we recruited participants by word of mouth, we tended to attract people similar in outlook. A common language tends to develop in such an instance, with certain "in" words and phrases marking us as a community. "You focus on your agreement so much, you may lose touch with the real differences," Ben warned.

The participants recognized that the low fees and the staff not deriving much income from the work were consistent with what we were teaching in the workshops about the place of money in finding one's calling. Ben cautioned that we needed to rethink "living by faith as verification of what we are doing." Perhaps he was conscious of a subtle tendency toward spiritual hubris in our strong belief in doing outside work to support the ministry. Temptations are subtler for those engrossed in occupations seen as "spiritual." Attention must be paid.

3. WHAT IS THE PSYCHOLOGICAL IMPACT OF THE STAFF ON THE CHARACTER OF THE WORK?

The evaluation that may have made the most impact on us as founders was focused on the three of us on staff. Ken Larsen, director of Clinical Pastoral Education at Danvers Mental Hospital, psychologist and clergy person, carried it out in 1985. First, we each wrote a personal autobiography to help Ken locate us in our vocations. Then Ken met separately with Dick, Don and me. Finally, he convened a meeting to present his findings and counsel to us.

His findings were full of resonant wisdom for the three of us. As a psychologist, Ken read our autobiographies with insight. He saw, far more clearly than we did, the extent to which our movement into the ministry of Life/Work had hidden roots in our unrecognized reaction to experiences we were leaving behind. He wrote:

> The three staff persons came together at respectively painful terminations of creative ministry endeavors: Dick with the bankruptcy of Many Mansions, and Don and Eunice with their decision to leave the Urban Life Center in Chicago. From their stories, I conclude that a strange combination of grief, dependency needs, and yet untapped creative impulses and love for urban ministry drew them together to form Life/Work Direction.

This indicated to him our need to redefine our goals and reasons for continuing this ministry. He compared it to a marriage. "The reasons why one gets married are more than likely not the reasons why one stays married. Now, as the organization matures, projections must be withdrawn and integrated on an individual basis."

Ken's major contribution had to do with assessing the powerful impact the three of us had on participants by virtue of our particular qualities. He brought to our attention "the reality of the power shadow in the helping professions."[21] He wondered how unsophisticated, less defended and more vulnerable participants might experience "the collective power of this dynamic threesome." More important, he suggested we "become even more conscious of the personal roles projected onto [us] of mother, father, knower of everything," as well as the religious symbolism as "dispenser of God's grace, protector from God's wrath, and healer of their bodies and souls." He wanted us to be "strong enough to carry these projections when they exist, but never to identify unconsciously with these roles."

I remember hearing these wise observations soberly. I saw that by maintaining a presence separate from the protection of any sponsoring institution, we were exposed and vulnerable. Our charisms were just that—gifts of grace. No wonder we kept reaching out to advisors who would speak truth to us and require that we respond with candor and honesty in return.

One outcome of the evaluation process itself was the ability to define more precisely the subtle difference in our ways of working. We talked about this as staff and in a letter to our members, we shared our thoughts about what we had learned:

> There are ways in which our varied gifts and styles conflict. Don commented, "People have to get used to us." Eunice added, "We are affected by each other's gifts, learning from one another, leaving room in our approach for one another."

We began to understand some of the weaknesses as well as strengths, the possible pitfalls as well as potentials of this particular three-person entity. We are constantly reminded of our relationship to the Trinity who is God, of our connection to the source of power, or how our focus internally is related to our mission outwards. Our propensity for ongoing self-study and evaluation continued informally through the years. At major turning points, the process became deliberate as we gathered a small group of selected advisors—people familiar with the work and interested in the way it was developing—to glean their wisdom and combine it with our own perspectives.

Two turning points—a geographic move in 1990 and Dick Faxon's impending retirement in 1993—underlined our need to surround ourselves with steady counsel and support by adding members to our board. Not surprisingly, we turned to Carmel and John Cuyler to be the first non-staff members of the board. They knew our history, and they were invested in the future of the work. Others joined for a time through the 1990s and beyond. As a ragtag and independent outfit in many respects, we needed to be accountable. We chose members carefully, wanting both supportive advice and good questions. We were not a conventional nonprofit, operating with an impersonal board. Our choices were personal, based on friendship and trust, typical of our organizational style with its corresponding assets and deficits.

The writing of this book is in itself a form of evaluation. As I write, I am turning the spotlight onto our process as a ministry. I am learning to see our formation in new ways, noting the continuities and the discontinuities. I ponder the reasons for our decisions and the direction we took. I unearth anecdotes from the files and share them with our present staff to compare notes with what "we have always done" and what fresh ways of thinking are emerging.

I call to mind times when things went awry. I think it was our thirty-fourth group in 1985 that fell apart one-third of the way through the workshop. Three members formed a resistant clique that argued with the group and with us and opted out, leaving the other three group members disappointed but determined to continue. I don't remember how we processed this, but it made us more vigilant in accepting new participants to ensure they were in harmony with the approach we offered. We were careful when prospective participants were referred by their therapist, and seemed to lack the necessary stability to take on the kind of process we offered. We also were not set up to deal with the hard core unemployed. We learned to honor our limits.

The most common criticism had to do with disappointment that the process ended without the person having achieved their goal of a new job. Hard as we tried to make clear what we promised, not everyone wanted to "come apart" in all the ways we thought might be important—both in terms of taking time for an in-depth process and in allowing new spiritually-oriented perspectives on the issue of calling itself to emerge.

We also became accustomed to participants being reluctant to bring the process to an end. One of them said it flatly: "You are not very good at endings." It is true, we had grown to love each participant, and a bond had been established. Over time, we detected a hunger on the part of people to plow a deeper furrow in their quest for meaning in their life and they wanted to have our companionship in that quest. That is when we began making part of the final session an invitation to return for further work. Now they could set their own agenda, based on any unfinished business they perceived. This led to people returning periodically over the years for free-flowing sessions, as well as for spiritual guidance in various forms as we offered them.

We do not fit neatly into the classification of an educational institution with an ordered curriculum. The nature of the work is more readily identified as organic—meaning a living entity "consisting of elements that exist together in a natural relationship that makes for organized efficiency."

May it be so, and may there always be both life and direction in this work to which we are called.

PART THREE

Establishing a Direction

interweaving others' callings

*"The whole body, joined and knit together,
as each part is working properly, promotes the
body's growth in building itself up in love."*
Ephesians 4:16

CHAPTER 10

Bringing Life/Work Home:
envisioning a larger tapestry

In the spring of 1990, we wrote these words in our newsletter:
> We have begun to think about finding a place for Life/Work Direction which would be more of a home environment, and which would include living quarters for Don and Eunice. The idea is in an embryonic stage, but we share it with you as a way of networking, in case you have knowledge of possible places. We see such a move as two or three years away—but one never knows.

No, one never knows. We were pleasantly surprised a few days later when Scott Walker came by. He and his wife, Louise, were planning to buy a house as they awaited the birth of their first child. They offered to buy a two-family house in order to share it with Life/Work Direction and with Don and me.

It felt natural to us for Scott and his wife to be the ones to respond to our plea. We knew Scott from his frequent visits to our storefront. We had done the first stages of pre-marital counseling for Scott and Louise before their wedding in 1987. We had encouraged Scott in pursuing his calling in education. Jamaica Plain seemed like a logical choice of location, standing halfway between the Walkers' Dorchester church, to which they had a strong connection, and Scott's job at Brookline High School.

※

The four of us set out together to find a place that would house our two families and Life/Work Direction. We were an odd coupling—Don and I sporting our broad-brimmed straw hats, Louise pregnant and in her billowing jumper, and Scott still dressed in his teaching garb. We tramped

Scott and Louise Walker at the threshold of their home on Halifax Street.

along after the realtor, checking out the few available properties deemed suitable. Last on the list was 32 Halifax Street. I was hesitant at first, having previewed it and found it strange and unappealing, standing out from its environment like a sore thumb. The house occupied a corner lot and looked like a triple-decker laid on its side, and was flanked with so many windows, I stopped to count them. Thirty-two in all to keep washed and clean! The realtor was intent on showing us this house and Louise was equally insistent. She saw the symbolism in those windows, "a way to see in and to see out," she said, "and in tune with the seasons, a time for being open and a time for closing."

Stepping inside, we were instantly won over by the magical interior design. We loved the inviting entrance, the beamed ceilings, the gumwood paneling, the fireplace and its mantel, and the natural division between work space on one side and living quarters on the other. The Walkers would make their home on the top two floors, and Life/Work Direction would share the ground floor with Don and me. As Louise put it, "We found the house only to discover as the years went on that it would be the house that found us."

We were just beginning to know Louise, for whom this move had particular significance. Her love for community was embedded in her life experience and core to her way of being in the world and would sweeten the way we inhabited the space. She related to us her history of living in community:

In Louise's words

I had grown up in community because my dad was headmaster and teacher at boarding schools. I used to spend my summers volunteering at the FOCUS Study Center (Fellowship of Christians in Universities and Schools) where I lived with high school kids. After college, I took a job at Emma Willard School in the Berkshires, where once again I lived among high school girls, followed by three years working with junior high students at a boarding school in

Southern California. Then I returned to the East Coast to do youth ministry for four more years.

Around the time I got married, I moved to Boston and began trying to find my place in the city. In my quest for community, I entered the Clinical Pastoral Education program at Boston City Hospital. Because I was living in Dorchester, and needed to be close to what I loved as well as what I was afraid of, I chose to work on the ward with gunshot victims, where I could be close to the people and be immersed in their stories. I was both challenged and fed. I began to wonder about pursuing hospital chaplaincy. That thought would be stored in my heart because in the final months of the program I discovered I was pregnant.

I think it was fitting that it was the upcoming arrival of Samuel—whose name means "God has heard"—that brought us together. Don and Eunice had prayed to find a place for their work, and it turned out to be this pregnancy that opened the door for them and for us.

Scott and Louise's instinct for community warmly touched us. I will never forget my startled response the first time Louise knocked on our door to borrow a cup of sugar. My years of anonymous urban living had made me forget that such neighborly gestures still exist. All my childhood associations from life in small town New England bubbled to the surface. We become neighbors when we share the staples of life. Suddenly, Don and I knew we had much more than the brick and mortar of a shelter from the weather; we had community. The Walkers' generosity of spirit permeated our relationship.

My initial focus was on the significance of this move for our work. I felt we were standing on the threshold of a long-held dream. We recognized God's hand in it, yet even in this, neither the Walkers nor the three of us in Life/Work Direction grasped the full import of our move. We could not envision what was in store—interweaving the sturdy threads of Life/Work Direction with the life force and calling of the Walkers.

༄

We had some worries about no longer being located conveniently near a subway and wondered if people from Cambridge and Dorchester would be able to make their way to us. The beauty of the tree-arched Jamaicaway leading uphill from the Fenway area toward our home sometimes presented a challenge to drivers with its hazardous sharp twists and turns.

The surrounding quiet neighborhood shaded by tall trees was a stark contrast to what we had left behind in Dorchester. Would the setting be too imposing for our clientele? There was ample parking space in front, an amenity to be prized in Boston.

We made a home for Life/Work Direction in the downstairs space by turning the dining room into work space, placing that beloved round table from the Dorchester storefront directly under the chandelier. The china cabinet became our storage space for supplies. We filled each of the rectangular cabinet windows with our favorite photographs, art pieces, and bright sayings. The living room with its gumwood paneling and fireplace became the "Common Room" for gatherings apart from the work. We decided against trying to make the fireplace workable, and placed a piano on the hearth instead. We installed a lavatory for guests in a corner off the hallway. A table with all the makings for hot tea welcomed guests in the entryway.

Shortly after settling into this new environment, I wrote these words in my journal one morning:

It is the darkness before dawn and I come awake, listening to a soft rainfall outside the window here at the house. Soon I get up and move down the corridor, sensing the spaces as I pass, in the dim light from a street lamp outside.

The prayer book lies open on the hassock in the Common Room where the three of us had left it the night before, at the end of an evening of seeing people. I move on into the sunroom/office, now shadowy and still.

The faint stirrings from the floor above remind me that someone is preparing for a day of work and also that a baby will be born in this house within the next month or two.

I feel the Birth of our Life, our Work, and the Direction of both—in new ways—graced by this gift of space. It gently presses us into a new mold, a new way of living and being, and must affect the work we do here. I cannot live too close to my work, occupy this kind of space, without tasting deeply of gratitude and integrity. Gratitude because of the kindness and beauty of the place. Integrity because of presence and transparency.

We called on Curtis Almquist, our spiritual director at the SSJE monastery, to come down and conduct a House Blessing. By the time this took place, Louise was cradling their son Sam in her arms as we gathered together to consecrate the space to God for the ministry to which we felt called. We included the Walkers' space upstairs as well, recognizing their common commitment to living life as God's servants. The whole house was dedicated. We had learned from the realtor that the previous occupants had conducted a house church on the top floor of this structure! It had been a kind of seal on the Walker's decision to make an offer on the house.

Dick was very clear in seeing the house as a home, symbol of a household community. He made his patient way from Cambridge using the circuitous route necessary by Red Line subway and Green Line trolley and bus without complaint. He was planning to retire in a few years and was beginning to shift his attention toward the future.

❦

The move of Life/Work Direction to a home had deeper resonance for me than is apparent on the surface. My life experience had been one of frequent moves, starting with my birth into a minister's family that often inhabited a church manse wherever my father became pastor. I adapted readily to our family's nomadic existence and the various houses we occupied. After I left home, this pattern continued for two decades, first in rented rooms with kitchen privileges followed by a series of apartment rentals shared with other single women—collecting the orange crates and makeshift brick and board bookcases and odd-lot fabrics for bedspreads typical of those times. It was a life style typical of my peers, and I had no cause for complaint.

It turned out that my lifestyle and work choices would never lend themselves to the kind of stability and focus that accompanies home ownership, maintenance and repair. When I married, it turned out that neither Don nor I would be willing to bring in the kind of income to support a down payment, and when it came to taking care of a house, Don and I were klutzes. As Don once famously crowed, "Fix things? I can't even screw in a nail!" (Or was that "hammer a screw"?)

The house at 32 Halifax Street would not be ours, but it symbolized something important to me—security in a welcoming environment and a place to plant our feet for the foreseeable future. The owners were persons who saw this venture as creating community and not just investing in real estate. This gave our occupancy a different feel. One of my first delights was planting flowers in window boxes in the spring. Later Don and I contracted with a landscape architect to add shrubbery to the lawn. On one of the hottest days in July, we hired a lovable Irish mason who came at dawn and worked all day to construct stonework to beautify the steps leading to the front entrance.

It was not in the Walkers' nature to take on an imposing landlord role, nor did they treat us like tenants. We would be the ones to raise the rent periodically, install new kitchen cupboards, and suggest changes for which we helped pay. At the same time, we could not care for the physical plant when it needed repairs, and they were faithful in doing this. It was an ideal partnership. They were God-sent "angels" to us.

The house on Halifax Street became home—and our work place. The combination of functions introduced a familiar dimension. As in so many other aspects of the Life/Work Direction operation, our personal and professional lives were inextricably intertwined. There are both hazards and comforts in such a mingling of life and work and not everyone would find it comfortable or wise. For some reason, Don and I seem to have the temperaments to maintain good boundaries. We move from the work space to our more private area easily, closing the "mental door" on our last session of the day. Perhaps my years in the parsonage as a child accustomed me to the idea that deep work with someone could take place in our family living room.

For Don, the move made life seamless. He immediately was delighted with "the commute" and joked that now he could find his way to work without getting lost. He reveled in the unity of life and work that our new home provided him because he took this opportunity to stop working at his outside jobs and settled firmly into creating a space that fostered both his life as a poet and his work as counselor to participants in the vocational process.

Innocently and eagerly, we placed our eclectic mix of furniture everywhere—like the bookcases that used to be shoebox shelves from our days at Many Mansions. Up on the wall went favorite paintings and photographs along with objects originating from participants. Most of the furnishings were scavenged from sidewalk gleanings on garbage days or from a yard sale or thrift store. Despite the fact that we were thereby placing our characteristic stamp on the décor, neither of us ever felt proprietary ownership of the first floor. The space was more identified in our minds as the location of Life/Work Direction than our personal habitat. Living there was a gift.

It made a difference that the Walkers owned the house, lived upstairs, borrowed sugar occasionally, and shared car use with us. We felt understood, provided for, cared about; and yet maintained a discreet and delicate separateness that preserved the kind of communal sensibility that made it possible to share the same house with equanimity and trust. The Walkers began developing a seasonal rhythm in their lives—Scott teaching school all year, and then spending summers on Martha's Vineyard as host family for eight college students attached to a program familiar to them—FOCUS (Fellowship of Christians in Universities and Schools), an organization that maintains a non-coercive presence in private schools to help students explore the reality and adventure of a life of faith. Every fall, the Walkers returned with lively tales of their summer ministry to share with Don and me.

Slowly, over the years, a vision for ministry was emerging upstairs and would find its way over the threshold of the door into our downstairs hallway. In the beginning this was not foreseen. It would happen when all of us were ready.

CHAPTER 11

On the Threshold:
adding colorful new threads

1990-2005

WE MOVED TO JAMAICA PLAIN—such a simple statement rolls off my tongue, disguising the import of the changes taking place. Don and I were the most oblivious, since we were nestling into a secure home space for the long term. The move looked quite different to Dick who was turning sixty-five in three years and had begun to talk about retirement.

At first Don and I ignored this; then a past participant in one of our first workshops, Joe Verla, came by one day to talk and called our attention to the impending change that Dick's retirement would bring. He had a natural inclination to reach out to Dick, having been deeply affected a decade before by early morning counseling and prayer sessions with him. Now he wanted to reach out protectively to ease Dick's transition into retirement. He was concerned to find ways for Life/Work Direction to continue steadily without Dick's integrative presence. "You can't replace Dick," he cautioned.

We began to assess what we would be losing when Dick retired. The three of us represented a unique balance in terms of basic energies: head, heart and gut. Dick was the thinker, I was the feeler, and Don operated by gut instinct. We were going to miss those thoughtful questions Dick always brought to the table. We would miss the banter, the stimulating arguments, and his witty observations. The fact that he had a separate life in Cambridge and came from outside the house added a refreshing dimension to each day. We would miss him, but we also recognized that he was ready to embark on a more leisurely chapter of life with his wife, Alicia.

To mark Dick's leaving in a special way, we decided on a celebration for his sixty-fifth birthday in September, 1992. Don suggested we call it a Bar Mitzvah, honoring Dick's thirteen years of ministry beginning with Many Mansions. It was planned in elaborate detail by a cadre of participants eager to honor Dick. Joe Verla put together the beginning liturgy of Evensong. Three talented musicians—Jan Curtis, opera singer; Chris Greco, playwright; and Pam Kristan, accompanist—interwove a series of songs with appropriate commentary by Dick tracing his years of ministry, evoking vivid imagery.

Then Dick rose to share a heartfelt homily in the tender way characteristic of him, ever the priest. It was followed by a wave of appreciative responses from people in the audience, moderated by John Cuyler, who with his wife, Carmel, was now on our board. Their upfront presence signaled to everyone gathered that Life/Work Direction was now in the hands of a group of five, not just the three staff. Carmel presented Dick with a gift, a hand-sewn wall hanging of the Life/Work Direction logo, the mandorla. Scott Walker was present that night too, attempting to record everything on tape for posterity.

Down in the basement afterwards, we served homemade cakes. During a brief interlude, we narrated a slide presentation depicting the adventurous early days of Many Mansions. Pam Kristan led us in a ritual circle dance that gave us a graceful way to say hello and goodbye to each other before we walked out into the night. An era was passing, though we did not articulate it at the time.

We said a final goodbye to Dick in a special walk around Jamaica Pond joined by Life/Work friends in May, 1993. The transition was smooth as Don and I settled into the rhythm of our days. We complemented each other easily and seamlessly, reading each other's signals governing the pace of each session. We missed a particular grace Dick possessed. Dick had been the one slower to respond in sessions, but when he did contribute his wisdom, it exuded authoritative power. Without Dick, participants were faced with two active listeners. Don and I deliberately developed a style of open confrontation with each other as a way of defusing any assumption that we represented a united front. This opened up space for the participant to enter the conversation as an equal with the two of us. Don could make a provocative statement, while I was often the one to hold back, leaving space for reflection or a countering view.

This required a subtle shift in my way of listening, indicative of my increasing attention to the inner journey of the soul—my own and that of others. It was expressed most clearly in the new brochure we developed at the time with our graphic designer, Janet Piggins, who had also been with us as a participant. She came up with a striking new design with the title "Inner Journeys" across the cover. I felt she had captured the essence of our work as it had evolved. The lines I wrote inside the brochure describing Life/Work Direction emphasized the combined spiritual and psychological aspects of a soul journey. This was a nuanced shift from previous descriptions where the work orientation was more dominant. The brochure also announced the new fee of $30 per session, up from $20, a practical change. Our new location was more costly, and we were now being paid as full-time employees.

All the while, upstairs in the house on Halifax Street a great deal was going on. Sam was born shortly after we all moved in, and Luke arrived two and a half years later. For some time, the Walkers were absorbed in the tasks of parenting—with all its joys and complexities. However, it was not long before Scott and Louise were beginning to see part of the meaning of their marriage as a shared calling in work. None of us foresaw how this would affect us; we were moving in parallel universes, connecting periodically in our shared use of the washer-dryer and work on the garden. Underneath, there were hints of a common perspective on ministry and in particular on the meaning of vocation. They describe in their own words how their vision evolved.

In Scott and Louise's words

FINDING A CORNERSTONE
Scott: In the first years of our marriage, beginning in 1989, we chose to spend part of our summer vacations on Martha's Vineyard volunteering at FOCUS programs for high school students. It was natural for us. We appreciated what FOCUS had provided us when we were teenagers, Louise was still missed and much loved as a former FOCUS staff member, and I enjoyed teaching and interacting with high school students. We also had an early sense that our partnership was meant for a domain beyond marriage alone.

We were not likely to create the kind of marriage where each partner goes his and her separate ways. We were good friends who worked well together and dreamed in pastoral ways. It was natural for Louise and me to imagine collaborating in ministry in some fashion. Along with leading a small group in our church, summer volunteering with FOCUS gave us a place to explore our capacity as a couple.

These stints of summer volunteering in a two-week high school program eventually led to a proposal from FOCUS leaders that struck us as crazy, yet wonderful. In 1993, in the winter of my seventh year of teaching at Brookline High School, we were asked to consider dedicating eight weeks of the summer to hosting and leading a household community for college students. While the students worked summer jobs on Martha's Vineyard, we would help them to grow spiritually and to integrate their faith with their work experience and community life. We would receive room and board but no pay. From one angle, the idea seemed outrageous: our two year old son Sam required our attention, Louise was eight months pregnant with Luke and this FOCUS assignment would swallow most of our free summer time.

Even so, we found the offer arresting. Compelling possibilities offset the risks and anticipated losses. We had experienced enough in our marriage to recognize that we enjoyed and were creative in situations like this, building relationships and working informally with young people using daily life experience as our palette for teaching. The years of working in separate worlds during the day made the chance to collaborate in this way too promising to pass up. It was a job description, albeit volunteer, with our names and sense of potential written all over it.

The college house was called Cornerstone, a fitting name for the role it came to play in our development. It gave us an incomparable gift: eight summers of daily give-and-take with students around the typical issues twenty-year-olds face—job hunting, dealing with employers, navigating short-term romantic episodes, and resolving conflict with each other over household tasks of cooking and cleaning. On a deeper level, we grappled with the meaning of being "in the world but not of it" and figuring out what God has to do with the exigencies of everyday life. We found that there was something distinctly different and powerful in working as a couple and in teaching from life experience. Louise and I called it "the house of disillusionment," not for what it left us feeling, but for what it offered students who came with romanticized assumptions about Christian identity and community, and about marriage and child rearing.

From the start, Louise was entirely at home in this setting and role.

My experience required a surrender. As a classroom teacher accustomed to fifty-minute increments of relatively controlled exposure each day and evenings repairing to a private home where I refueled, living round the clock with students ushered me well beyond my comfort zone, especially for two months running. While we did use books and formal discussions, more than ever before, I needed to unbutton my professorial self and let my everyday relaxed self hang out with others.

I was amply satisfied and stimulated as a classroom teacher in social studies during these years. I found it challenging and rewarding, especially the creative process of curriculum development where I was drawn to the use of simulations and experiential activities and reflection. Nevertheless, after two or three summers, our experience at Cornerstone began to rival the fulfillment I found in the classroom. Working more intensively and relationally with a small group of students, blending my nature together with Louise's in complementary ways resulted in something powerful that trumped my most rewarding experiences at Brookline High School. We were clearly making a dynamic connection with these college students and many of them wanted to remain in touch with us, to keep talking and learning.

In fact, what began as a sideline pursuit became a place of epiphanies and disciplines that began to feed our imagination with a vision extending beyond the summer. A few Cornerstone practices were particularly prescient. We learned to love and use the life stories of characters from Scripture to help others recognize God's place within their own stories. Louise and I took regular, long walks with each student to keep the group experience grounded in individual responsibility for growth. It was characteristic of our style of working to make the celebration banquet on the final night a ritual that cemented the summer's experience for each person. We took recycled jars from our refrigerator, labeled each one decoratively with the name of each house member and with the verse "We have this treasure in jars of clay to show that this all surpassing power is from God and not from us." (II Corinthians 4:7) One at a time we passed the jars around the table allowing each member of the community to receive affirmations about his or her unique gifts and contributions to the house, spoken out and then placed in writing in their jar.

The balance of our life—a traditional family pattern during the school year, and intensive summer experiences with students—began to change. We started to bring Cornerstone home with us, at first by inviting some of these students to live with us in our home in Jamaica Plain as they explored their next steps after graduation.

Louise: Cornerstone proved to fulfill its name in our life, becoming the support for our unique calling. It gave us an opportunity to fully express ourselves in all dimensions: as a man and woman, as husband and wife, as mother and father, as counselor and teacher, and as companions on the pilgrimage of life.

I remember sitting around the lunch table with our interim pastor and his wife one fall, wondering aloud what our life would look like as time went on. We were already feeling the growing pains that Cornerstone had seeded in us. He looked at us intently, "Dear ones, God will give you what you are to do. It will come; only wait." Those were not the words we wanted, but they quieted us with a deep assurance.

A SABBATICAL CALLING

Scott: For us the waiting process took a particular form—a weekly Sabbath, something we were mercifully taught to value early in our marriage. I was caught in old patterns of overworking which my marriage brought painfully into view. When this came to a head in our second year, Louise challenged me to give God more room to prove his control and providence over my life as a husband and teacher. In that moment of crisis and challenge, something deep stirred in me, a call to healing and freedom that I long desired and knew was possible. The freedom came as we began walking out the Sabbath rest God promises.

And that's just what we did. We literally walked it out. On date nights on Sunday evenings, we walked for hours together. We loved walking. Something about the passage of time and scenery and the physical movement loosened perspective. It was on these long Sabbath walks that we reflected on treasures gleaned from our summer Cornerstone ministry and began to pray and dream into the future.

In 1996, after ten years of teaching and in the middle of our Cornerstone years, I decided to take a full "sabbatical" year from my high school post to sort out these stirrings toward change. Officially it was an unpaid "leave of absence" that allowed me to return to Brookline High School the next year if I wanted, though I felt sure that I would not go back. I worked on and off with a carpenter friend to make ends meet, enjoying the simplicity of physical labor that left room for reflection. Louise and I enjoyed having more time together and kept taking our Sabbath walks. At the end of one particular winter walk, we stopped at a café. Several fragments of inspiration came together in what felt like a complete vision for a yearlong program for recent college graduates. It would provide a way for them to benefit from internships and mentoring as they considered the unfolding direction of their lives. It was exciting. We rushed home to transfer napkin notes into a full outline of our vision.

A month later an avenue opened for us to advance this vision! Simon Barnes, the executive director of FOCUS, having seen the fruit of our work at Cornerstone, approached us to ask if we would become the directors of their College Ministry. It was a new wing of FOCUS' ministry in need of development, and the Cornerstone program would now be a part of the job description.

We considered the offer seriously. It was attractive, allowing Louise and me to collaborate in ways we had hoped, but given what was on our hearts, it needed more to win us. We agreed to take the job if FOCUS would also let us develop a post-college program along the lines of our vision designed to help recent graduates explore God's calling for their lives and work. The program would last through a school year and be based in Boston. It would be named Threshold. Simon and others were delighted with this idea, seeing it as a unique way to strengthen the college work. We agreed to take the position beginning in the late spring of 1997.

Something else important took place that sabbatical year: we attended a conference on Healing Prayer led by author Leanne Payne. The conference struck a deep chord in us. It offered a rich blend of psychological and theological perspectives on collaborating with God in the healing of the soul. Louise and I began to seek healing for the effects of wounds in our own family backgrounds—alcoholism in her family, and divorce in mine. Our experience at the conference was a home coming for us both. It launched a healing journey for us that continued for the next seven years through our leadership involvement in Living Waters, a program focused on healing relational and sexual brokenness. These experiences combined to influence the way we approached our work with young adults, a work that laid importance on confronting the brokenness of old claims upon a person's identity.

THE SHAPE OF THRESHOLD

After assuming our new post with FOCUS, we worked through 1997 and into 1998 establishing a variety of initiatives for the college ministry. We made no effort to develop a school-based presence, knowing that other organizations provided ample opportunities for Christian fellowship and growth on campuses. Instead we trained our energies on preparing FOCUS students for three key transitions: the transition into college which often took a toll on their faith; the transition into leadership as volunteers in FOCUS' programs for younger students; and of special interest to us, the transition into the world after college graduation for which we were nursing the vision for Threshold. While raising funds for our salaries, we began working on each of these fronts.

In the spring of 1998, we called together a small group of advisors in Boston, enterprising friends experienced in student ministry and in creating and developing organizations. We presented to them a vision statement for Threshold that included the following:

> *Program Aim* — To help young adults (especially recent college graduates) develop a coherent and compelling vision for living out their faith in the world through a multifaceted experience of mentoring within the Body of Christ in Boston.
>
> *Program Rationale* — When Jesus first called his disciples, we are told that he "appointed twelve,...that they might *be with him* and that he might *send them out*." (Mark 3:14, emphasis ours). From the beginning, preparation for sending out into the world involved simply being with the Master. The example of Jesus is as pertinent today as ever, especially for young adults. In our society the transition from college to working life is a critical period for testing and establishing vision for how life is to be lived. Whether beliefs are discarded or remain, and how much the remainder shapes the formation of a way of life can be influenced greatly by the living models of belief that a person is afforded during this key transition period.

We described our vision in terms of the people served, the program offered, and the place where we would meet with them.

The People

We envisioned a coed program of as many as ten students with a deliberate mix of ethnic and socio-economic backgrounds. We wanted participants to encounter the range of God's presence and concerns in the world through the diversity of each other's life experiences. We knew we could recruit participants from the mostly white, upper middle class world of FOCUS, and our leadership within our inner-city church and Boston Living Waters program gave us a platform for recruiting a wider range of young adults from the city. We designed the program with the just-out-of-college person in mind. Over time we would recognize that Threshold attracted a slightly older set eager to reflect on their experience after initial forays into the world had left them restless or disillusioned.

The Program

Mentoring was at the heart of our vision and initially this led us to imagine a program based on four main pillars: internships in the community, participation in a local church, study and reflection as a group through lectures, workshops, and discussions, and life together in one household. As our thinking developed, the study and reflection pillar became central, and we incorporated our other values within it. The program would feature:

- discussion of contemporary books and classics that explore the Christian notion of vocation and the challenge of integrating faith and work;
- theological reflection on several of the great life stories from Scripture to gather insights into the experience of calling;
- interaction with a variety of people from the Boston area whose lives speak to the reality of being led by God to interesting intersections of their giftedness and the needs of their community;
- engagement in exercises designed to aid participants in identifying gifts and motivations, some of the same creative exercises I appreciated in my own Life/Work Direction experience;
- seasonal retreats through which the central themes of the program would be progressively introduced in innovative ways that incorporated the arts.

Louise: I was particularly excited about the idea of inviting guest speakers to address the group. We were part of an eclectic Bible study group at the church we attended in Dorchester. They were people with colorful life stories and the wisdom of life experience to share. We wanted our young participants to connect with people of widely differing characteristics—in age, ethnicity, socio-economic class, professional lives, and church background. From the beginning, we prized diversity, knowing how homogeneous the college experience can be. We wanted to break down barriers of race and class through natural human contact.

Scott: Though the idea of internships was compelling, we scrapped it. Not only was it difficult to secure internships of the quality we wanted, but also we recognized that many candidates for Threshold would need to remain in jobs, leaving them little time to engage in an internship experience. We preserved the spirit of experiential learning by creating a final field assignment that required Threshold participants to explore their vocational interests in the world by interviewing potential mentors in various fields.

We encouraged participation in local churches and initially created a lengthy church profile to help those who came from out-of-town. We knew the value of being rooted in a community of faith both for support and for perspective in recognizing one's gifts and abilities through service. Later we would find that a substantial proportion of Threshold participants came to us struggling with their church affiliation and needing the freedom to step back from church activities to reassess their place in the Body of Christ. We provided a safe place and way to reexamine their relationship to the church.

The Place

One of our initial ideas was to base the program in a residential experience. We were used to Cornerstone, a place where we could live with the persons who came to be with us in the program. We had our eyes on a house near our home, and even engaged in conversations with a real estate broker, but we soon felt that the house was becoming too important. Over several months of planning and through a trip to observe a program in Washington D.C. that involved similar goals, we decided against this approach.

Louise: We realized we were not to create an experience for the participants in a protected residential environment, but rather we were to go with their experience as they moved into the city and be there for them as they encountered life and work every day. For all that could be gained through a shared community life, we saw the disadvantages of prolonging their college dorm experience. We wanted to work alongside young adults as they faced the realities of finding affordable housing, and of getting along with housemates, rather than manage these things for them.

I had the image of the boxing coach who, after each round, towels the guy off and sends him back in for another round. Other more experienced persons warned us that a residential experience doesn't equip a person to stand strong in the midst of countervailing forces. Simply walking alongside Threshold participants was itself a significant offering for us to make.

We would seek to build a sense of community in other ways, by beginning our group meetings with a meal in our home—replicating some of the earthy family feel that had been generated at Cornerstone, where our sons, Sam and Luke, sat around the dinner table, too. Through our experiences in healing ministries we knew the sacramental power of the dinner table where God's shalom blessing was symbolized in a visceral way. We also hoped the seasonal retreats in a place apart would bond us all together.

Scott: These were the core ideas that we presented that night in the spring of 1998 to our circle of advisor friends. The group reacted with instantaneous enthusiasm. One member burst out, "Just start! Do a pilot! Then tell people about what you have already done." That convinced us that running a pilot was a better way of gathering financial support than just writing a proposal about future plans. Six months later in the fall of 1998 we convened our first Threshold group.

One of the members of that advisory circle was Stephanie Smith (now Choo), who appeared on Life/Work Direction's doorstep in 1981 with a quest similar to Scott's, wanting to find a way to express her faith meaningfully. Her response to the Walkers' proposal was instant and heartfelt:

I was immediately intrigued by what the Walkers proposed. I had known them for many years, and had seen firsthand how gifted they were in helping young people come home to themselves and into a more authentic relationship with God. I suggested that the three of us get together once a week to talk and pray about this venture. A few years before I had helped friends as they launched a new organization by coming alongside them and asking questions, helping them shape and refine their ideas. I began to see that this was a core gift of mine, and I wanted to offer the same support to the Walkers.

Initially I saw myself only as an advisor, but as we moved forward, I realized I wanted to be directly involved in the pilot project launched in the fall of 1998. The three of us so enjoyed the experience of working together the first year that the Walkers gladly welcomed me to continue. For the next five years, I worked alongside Scott and Louise as they created the Threshold project. Often the support I provided was practical—scheduling meetings, preparing for retreats, and other administrative tasks. At times the support was programmatic—I led a journal making workshop at our fall retreat, which proved to be a creative and integrating activity for participants as they were in the midst of telling and listening to life stories. In addition, my status as a single woman drew some Threshold women to identify with me and seek me out for counsel.

I was a listener and responder—debriefing with Scott and Louise after our meetings with participants, and continuing to ask questions as they shaped the program curriculum. We became a team of three in those developmental years, bringing different gifts and perspectives. I see now that in some ways we were like the Life/Work Direction threesome of Don, Eunice and Dick, a married couple with a third person who provided perspective, insight and encouragement.

Don and I, living and working downstairs, took note of the sounds of new life appearing on the doorstep each Wednesday evening when a group of twenty-something-year olds went trooping up the stairs for the evening Threshold meeting. Occasionally we looked in on the gathering, as invited. The atmosphere was warm and lively, a fresh wind reminiscent of our own years in Chicago working with slightly younger college students. We watched from a distance for several years before the need for new roots for Threshold appeared.

In Scott and Louise's words

Louise: In 1999, after three years of leading FOCUS' college ministry, we began feeling pulled in too many different directions between parenting, the Threshold program and other responsibilities of the college ministry. What was toughest was the travel we had to do for various college programs and FOCUS staff meetings. Since Scott and I were both involved, it was hard for us as parents. We began to pray about our future direction. We didn't know how such a change might take place, but we felt a need to be more stationary for a season. Our boys were older now, and not as portable as they once were. All along our boys have been like the Good Shepherd's "rods" leading us. Luke's six-year-old comment one day emphasized this. "Mom, I just want you to work at CVS so that I know where you are." CVS was one block from our house.

We began to pray for a way to bring our ministry home. We decided in faith to take on Threshold full time but turn over the rest of the FOCUS college ministry to others. The organization graciously agreed to serve as a conduit for the financial support that we needed to raise for the Threshold work in exchange for our willingness to serve in a pastoral role with FOCUS staff members.

Scott: This meant that we were now running Threshold as a "project" separate from the rest of the FOCUS ministry, but still administratively tied to FOCUS. Gradually we felt a need to find a more suitable organizational home for our work. We were grateful to FOCUS for launching and sustaining us as we began Threshold but we knew that our vision and goals were tangential to theirs.

In 2004, seven years after beginning Threshold, we took another sabbatical. We wanted to honor and explore God's command to give the land rest in the seventh year. During this sabbatical we began investigating options to incorporate Threshold or to link it with another ministry that would be a more fitting home.

Louise: We found we fit everywhere, but we didn't belong anywhere. The people we asked for advice about incorporation presented it in a way that made it seem cumbersome and complicated. We found other ministries that might extend an arm to embrace us, but it was clear to us that Threshold would be an extension, an implant. One day, in despair over our future direction, I came downstairs and sat at the table in Life/Work Direction's workspace and poured out my woes. Eunice and Don were sitting across from me. Suddenly Eunice erupted: "Why don't you come with us?'"

This accorded with our own instincts, led by God. We had poured our lives into the work at Cornerstone, and then Threshold, for more than ten years, reaching out to others. Now we heard God saying, "Let them come to you." And Eunice's invitation was just that.

Being part of Life/Work Direction would mean we would not be shouldering all the administrative burden of our work alone. We would be part of a team where the setup itself provided boundaries and limits that we needed.

Scott: This invitation meant that we had literally come home. Life/Work Direction had no ill-fitting pieces, for we were about the same mission. Our ways were different—we were more informal, for example—but we welcomed the order and structure, the solidity of what had been established. And in addition, we had the support of Don and Eunice, two persons experienced in this kind of ministry. And they attached no strings to the invitation. We settled into the embrace of Life/Work Direction gratefully.

That embrace turned out to be mutual. From the summer of 2005 to the present, the four of us crossed a threshold into a fascinating five-year process of entwining the strands of our lives and work. Each step along the way would be deliberate, and there would be adjustments and questions, laughter and tears, missteps and spontaneous leaps. We were very much in need of the touch of the Divine master weaver, who apparently had us in mind all the way.

Four energies merge to create Life/Work Direction for a new generation

CHAPTER 12

Becoming One in the Spirit:
blending colors into a new pattern

2005-2010

WE EMBARKED ON THE INTRICATE TASK OF INTERWEAVING the callings of the four of us. Looking at the tapestry of the work from the back, the strong colors Don and I had contributed over twenty-five years created a basic pattern, making the bright new threads introduced by Scott and Louise stand out with promise. The process of weaving the strands together harmoniously would take time.

We welcomed the fresh energy and felt the shape-shifting taking place in subtle ways as well as overtly. We wondered what would be retained in the fabric of Life/Work Direction and what would change, or disappear. The four of us embarked on a series of in-depth conversations where we opened ourselves up to each other and shared our deepest convictions about our callings. The result was the remarkable discovery of strong bold threads of commonality that would make a sturdy fabric possible. The foundations were solid, even as the Walkers brought gifts and perspectives that spoke to a new generation. We could weave old and new together, resting on principles we held in common.

THE COMMON THREADS:
THE WHY, THE WHAT, AND THE HOW

The Spirit of our Vision: the WHY
It was abundantly clear from our conversations in those first days in the Dorchester storefront that following Jesus was the first calling, taking priority over any sense of the calling to work in the world. The incentive

behind the Walkers' commitment to Threshold had a similar source: it exuded from their daily language and prayerful attitude of dependence on God. It was evident in the spiritually focused content of the curriculum they framed for Threshold. Louise's fresh personal way of being present to people in her sessions of Listening Prayer, and Scott's instinctive approach to group leadership were rooted and grounded in their attunement to Jesus' leading in every twist and turn of their life and work.

For all of us, finding one's calling has to do with choosing the over-all direction of one's life, and that choice is based on whom we choose to follow. Our process requires being with God in quiet attentiveness, for it is God who calls, "guiding us with His eye" as the Psalmist writes. Only then do we move with authority toward concrete action in the world of work.

The Concept of Calling: the WHAT
One aspect of our program that we knew we wanted to maintain was our concept of calling—that God calls us to become what we are, a unique expression of the Divine image. We would unearth this uniqueness by listening to participants tell us their story. Parker Palmer put it succinctly in the title of his book: *Let Your Life Speak*.[22] If a person's life is to speak, we need to attune our ears to listen to the story it tells.

We have found that stories contain the concrete stuff of lived experience out of which new decisions about life and work are made. Thankfully, the Walkers were equally dedicated to the use of story. We used storytelling throughout the curriculum to tease out the raw material of each participant's life. As the Walkers eased into place and picked up the Life/Work Direction vocational process with a few adaptations, they retained the use of stories as a central feature.

With the introduction of the Threshold program, the group mode was once again with us after twenty years' absence. We had missed this element. We were delighted that Scott's calling had always drawn him toward this mode, and its resulting sense of community. In the group setting, storytelling took on added dimensions. They explored the stories of characters in Scripture that illustrated the variety of ways a calling is experienced. Guest speakers were invited to tell the story behind their sense of vocation.

The work I had been doing in Spiritual Direction continued to be a solid chunk in the work. Now I was joined by Louise, whose special gifts in Listening Prayer had been honed in the preceding decade of experience. When requests came to Scott for direction, he began feeling his way into a form of spiritual guidance suited to his approach.

What emerged was a triptych of the vocational process and spiritual guidance for individuals, and Threshold for groups. This would have been a sufficient workload, except that we began getting requests for help from couples. In a way, this was a natural outgrowth of our work with individuals. It soon became clear that Scott and Louise had a particular gift for this work, one that matched the growing need in the culture for discerning support for marriages, both before and after the wedding.

Other new initiatives began spilling out from the Walkers' experience and gifts. They received requests from several churches, a school, and a not-for-profit ministry to lead retreats. These one- or two-day retreats were an ideal venue for examining stages in spiritual life and its expression in both life and work. The Walkers enjoyed creating lively exercises employing the senses, asking evocative questions stimulating thoughtful discussion, and encouraging informal communal storytelling. One request from a local church stimulated Scott to design a "Discovery Weekend" program introducing people to some of the exercises in the Life/Work Direction process. These weekends thus became a tool for recruitment to our longer-term work.

In all of these ways, we cherished the nature of the community that is bred by the intimacy of shared story at a crucial point of life/work transition. That point of change is where we are called to be.

The Educational Model of Transformational Learning: the HOW
Life/Work Direction is not a conventional educational institution; our model is more informal, closer to the contemporary concept of "transformational learning." Our primary goal is not to transmit a body of knowledge or even add new knowledge to an already conceived formulation of wisdom. Rather, we encourage participants to look at the ground of faith on which they stand and openly question it, free to examine assumptions and explore doubts. Faith is not simply something handed down by others; it has to become their own. We provide an educational setting where this kind of transformation can take place.

The four of us spent time together talking about the implications of this idea for our type of organization. Did we all come from this perspective of openness to change, even radical change? Could we find genuine freedom in our work with the new generation coming to our doors? The Walkers' response was reassuring. They were as concerned as we were about finding common ground with participants by using expressive and graphic language from contemporary life. "We're bilingual," Louise says. "We use living words." Like what happened at Pentecost, as we speak our words, we want participants to hear good news of God's love in their own language. Thus we meet participants on familiar ground and make it safe to be open to change. Scott finds that "it helps to incorporate imagery and artistic expression as part of the way we work. Use of the arts unsettles hardened assumptions and helps people listen to God afresh."

We continued drawing people who wanted a Christian context, but one where they could ask risky questions safely. We hoped they would find nurture here, but we did not want to lose a creative edginess that challenged them, something that had always characterized Life/Work Direction. Such an environment implies the freedom to call traditional perspectives into question—to rethink what they have been taught by parents and culture. At Cornerstone, the Walkers had worked through the challenge implied by the mixture of safety and risk in the environment they had created.

We were not trying to change others' *viewpoint,* but rather, their *point of viewing.* Taking on the "mind of Christ"—seeing as Christ sees, thinking as Christ thinks, and acting as Christ acts—breaks the shackles of a constrictive view of faith. In its place, we feel a new freedom in the Spirit. We are flooded with God's love, turning obedience into joy. In *The Naked Now,* Richard Rohr puts this kind of change dramatically, using the metaphor of technology:

> *You need a new motherboard, changing the actual hardware that processes your experiences. It is not merely a change of morals, group affiliation, or belief systems, but a change at the very heart of the way you receive, hear, and pass on your own experiences.*[23]

That, he says, is "transformative religion." Our educational model would not automatically produce this result; it could only open the way for something dynamically new to take place.

CHANGING SOME THREADS:
THE WHERE AND THE WHEREWITHAL

Space: the WHERE
Inviting the Walkers to join Life/Work Direction required some practical changes. The logical place to begin was with the allocation of work space. The Walkers felt relief in being able to make a distinction between their family life upstairs and work downstairs. Given the volume of people they were working with and their sons' needs, a clear boundary between the two areas of responsibility was needed.

Don instantly saw the importance of making a clear delineation between the work space up front, and our living space in the back. The thornier question had to do with the deeper implications of basing the work in a home. Don and I had lived with this anomaly for fifteen years, moving from bedroom to work space without giving it much thought. We now needed to clarify our identification with various spaces as personal or as pertaining to work.

We always saw the ground floor primarily as Life/Work Direction. Others saw it as our home. We worked hard to welcome the Walkers into the space, wanting them to fully occupy it for the work we hoped they could carry on. The Walkers moved forward slowly into ownership of the work area, deferring to our needs and wishes. They were just grateful to have a separate place to do their work and were awed by the sudden gift of having so much more space in their life than before.

We engaged in a dance together as, gradually, chair-by-chair, cupboard and bookcase and sofa and rug and copy machine and computer and files—everything found its place. Anyone coming in the door would charitably name our décor eclectic. The Walkers spiffed up the front entryway; the small lavatory we had added for guests a decade earlier now became even more essential; the Walkers' artistic touch in creating a rock garden and planting trees beautified the exterior; all of these gave the space its distinctive character.

Finances: The WHEREWITHAL
The Walkers would be raising their own financial support from donors committed to their previous ministry with FOCUS. We knew that our $30 fee per session would not be sufficient to support a couple with two children living in Boston in the twenty-first century! Raising the fee to $50 a session would help and was still modest, but we would need additional financial support. We saw that one way to define ourselves was as an educational institution to which students would pay tuition, and who might then become donors as alumni.

Alumni were already our major source of referrals. We didn't want to expend money on advertising or effort on marketing, as that would have required us to provide a pre-set mold, prescribed and articulated in detail and thus inevitably more superficial. Going by alumni referrals made us more confident that we would get participants who trusted our mode of working and wanted the depth and challenge we offered.

Over the years, some alumni did become long-term supporters of the work. A number of them gave donations designated to support other participants. In this way, the circle of financial support grew organically.

ADJUSTING THE TENSION ON THE LOOM:
ORGANIZATIONAL STRUCTURE AND IMAGE

The practical matters of organizational functioning proved easier to navigate: setting up clear arrangements for salary and medical coverage and purchasing liability insurance for the first time in our history, and drafting statements about possible conflicts of interest to protect us in areas related to ownership of the house.

The larger task was to figure out how this merger would create a fresh organizational structure. My initial image was not that of an umbrella with Threshold coming under Life/Work Direction's supervision, but rather an underlying foundation providing a legal and corporate base with the tax-exempt status essential for receiving financial support for the Walkers. Two parallel programs would rest on that base—Threshold and Life/Work Direction—with the board at the top. We were aware that the integrity of both parts needed to be preserved in the beginning.

By our second year, our common roots melded the parts together: the Threshold program for groups, and for individuals, the vocational process that had been the major hallmark of Life/Work Direction for twenty-five years, along with spiritual direction and Listening Prayer. At our annual board meeting in 2006, we were beginning to speak in a unified voice. Carmel intuited the change and articulated it in telling imagery:

> *Your speaking is a collective expression rather than a composite of Don/ Eunice's and Scott/Louise's thinking. What is happening now is different from the previous two years, when the partnership was like a bunch of sticks held together by a cord. Now the cord is no longer necessary because there is fertile ground beneath the partnership into which each staff member is sinking their roots and being sustained. The sticks have become plants, and the organization is growing.*

WHERE COLORS CONFLICT:
A NEW GENERATION, AND A NEW LANGUAGE

We continued to stay free of some aspects of institutionalization in order to be spare and agile enough to respond to the Spirit's movement in changing times. The people coming to us in 2010 are from a different generation and formed by a different culture than those in the 1980s.

Our historic stance of openness appealed to persons from many points on the religious spectrum. Some people came to us grounded in faith, others had an ambivalent or antagonistic attitude and were running away from it, and still others were without any foundation.

This always raised the question of language for us. How can we speak to the entire range of persons in terms they can grasp and that speak to their situation? The persons who first came to our storefront were saturated with Christian teaching and familiar with the Scriptures and the language of faith. We did not want to lose our moorings within our faith, but over time we began seeing participants who were more secular in their orientation. A growing number of participants were attracted to Eastern spiritual practices and were reluctant to use, or were offended by, terminology they connected with extreme or narrow views. There were "code words" in the culture that aroused suspicion about where we stood in relationship to popular Christian movements gaining ascendancy in the latter part of the twentieth century.

We had found it useful to think about a person's relationship to God in terms of *centered sets* versus *bounded sets*.[24] A bounded set mentality, characteristic of traditional evangelical thinking, pictures believers on one side of a fenced area, and unbelievers on the other side of the fence, totally separate. This mentality prompts us to try to convince a person to leap the fence by making a decision to believe in Christ. The person is either in the fold or a lost sheep outside.

Centered set thinking pictures God in the center of a vast area in which people stand at various distances from the center, and are either facing toward, or away from, the center. The idea here is that everyone is capable of movement toward or away from God, whether their location in the area is nearby (perhaps marked by a church affiliation) or distant (agnostic). This mindset made us look not so much at a person's location in relation to God at the center, but at the direction they are facing and the possibility of movement. When people came to us, we could ask genuine questions to which we did not have presumed answers. "What direction are you facing?" "What do you put your faith in?" We were looking for and encouraging movement toward God.

In the beginning of Threshold in 1998, the majority of participants came from an evangelical background familiar with the Scriptures and the language of personal faith. The Walkers were explicit about their own spiritual life, speaking freely of Jesus in a personal way. In joining us at Life/Work Direction, they encountered a more diverse group in terms of religious background and interest. Don voiced his concern that language common to the Walkers and former participants they served would be a barrier to people from the broader population that we had been reaching.

At the same time, the Walkers began noticing changes in the young people they were attracting, a new generation, engaged in mainstream culture—not countercultural like our 1980s participants. They might have a church background, but felt less intense loyalty toward it. They were not saturated with Scriptural teaching, and were more questioning, more comfortable with "not knowing." They might be active in a church but their engagement was understood more in personal and experiential terms and was less tied to religious institutions and doctrines.

All four of us had to look hard at our language and what it conveyed to our participants. For a time, we tiptoed around words with each other, looking for a robust language that held our faith in common. Don began realizing that he had lost touch with the initial raw vitality of our storefront conversations about following Jesus, in his eagerness to meet participants on their own ground. I felt a new freedom in rediscovering language soaked in Scriptural imagery and allusions. Its metaphorically rich language subverted antagonism toward religious clichés, bridging the gap between people of differing religious backgrounds and experience. Scott and Louise affirmed our "agreement in spirit," and were eager to expand their ministry beyond the Christian milieu familiar to them. They were grateful for the questions we posed to them from our broader experience. Where we all came together was in our openness to inquiry and lack of dogmatism. The centered set mentality helps us serve people wherever they are in their spiritual quest.

We now see both continuity and discontinuity between past and present in our approach. Our clientele in the twenty-first century comes from a changed culture from the 1980s, but because we remain on the margins of Christian institutions, we still constitute a safe place for genuine questions while at the same time providing a solid foundation exuding the faith, hope, and love that life in Christ promises.

WHAT EXPANDED AND DEEPENED:
ATTENTION TO THE INNER LIFE

When we began Life/Work Direction, my approach to the inner life was psychological, stemming from my life-changing therapy when I was 37. Yet I had attributed the miraculous change to God working through my therapist. The experience felt like a thread that intertwined the spiritual and psychological. My Protestant upbringing had tended to separate the two, and in fact some of my former peers were suspicious of therapy.

When I came to Boston and encountered Dick Faxon and the community at Many Mansions, I was put in touch with two sacramental traditions, Catholic and Episcopal, whose theology and liturgy put the emphasis not so much on a one-time conversion experience, but upon continuing relationship with God through the Eucharist and prayer. The words of Scripture—always so familiar to me—took on new dimensions in the setting of the liturgy. The way in which they were interwoven with rich hymnody and partaking of the sacraments evoked holy awe and spontaneous worship. I began rethinking the way I held my faith. There was more to it than I had tasted, and it made me hungry.

Even more compelling, both traditions contained a strong contemplative vein. Going on periodic silent retreats and having a spiritual director were new to me. My first weeklong retreat in 1983 made a crucial impact. I didn't know much about the place of silence in prayer, but I was an eager, if awkward, learner. I began reading the mystics—the poetry of St. John of the Cross and the autobiography of St. Theresa of Avila.

Above all, I discovered the writings of Thomas Merton, a Trappist monk, whose understanding of the inner life knit together my psychological explorations of the self with my relationship to God. This gave me another way of conceiving of the inner life. In therapy, I had uncovered what Merton calls my "true self"[25]—the person we are meant to be, made in the image of God. It ripped off the façade of the "false self"— my self-presentation as a Christian leader, struggling bravely to maintain a cheerful competent exterior. It freed me to confess my inner poverty of spirit, my dissatisfaction and misery with my life, my hypocrisy and illusions of who I was in others' eyes. I was absorbed with my unhappiness about being single. The spiritual sources I relied on in the past gave me little clue as to what was wrong, leaving me questioning why my faith in God did not seem to help. Therapy helped me face the truth about myself, and truth set me free to discover God in a way that felt radically new. It was transformational. I felt radiantly alive.

Through the first years of Life/Work Direction, I continued to explore the psychological realm in my reading and incorporate its insights into the way I worked with participants. Women began approaching me in our Dorchester storefront and asking me to work with them individually. My first instinct was to refer them to therapy. Very soon, Dick and Don told me, "These people are asking to work with you, Eunice." My initial reaction was, *"Moi?"* Then one day, a woman approached me and said, "Eunice, I don't know what you do, but whatever it is, I want to do it with you!" *Oh!* I thought.

It was at this point that I knew I had to begin a second track at Life/Work Direction in "spiritual direction"—the phrase we had providentially included in our founding charter. I sought out a spiritual direction peer group and began rethinking my calling. I found a supervisor, who was a former Carmelite monk as well as a Jungian analyst. My supervision sessions with him morphed into a full-blown analysis and a journey into the abyss of the dark night of my soul. It was another step in tearing the cover off any illusions I had that I could do spiritual work apart from total dependence on God.

Scott and Louise did their own psychological and spiritual exploration of the minefields that comprised their journeys from their families of origin to independent adulthood. It was marriage that thrust Louise into undiscovered depths in her soul. As a single woman, she felt the fullness of God and radiant happiness in her ministry with young people. Not long after her marriage to Scott, his pattern of overworking triggered hidden pangs of loneliness in Louise, reminiscent of her childhood in a home where her alcoholic parents had been emotionally absent. She had trained herself to work around their needs, ignoring her own pain. Now, in her despairing sadness and confusion, she looked for help from God. Being permanently committed to staying in her marriage, she felt trapped in an unhealthy dynamic. She had to trust that it would not be a betrayal to God to seek out counsel from a therapist.

She found in therapy that the psychological and spiritual did not clash, but meshed. She learned, "God loved me and gave me Scott to unearth what is deep in me." Others might offer a facile explanation: "Of course, as the child of alcoholic parents, you would marry an overworker." Louise saw it another way: Scott's pattern of overwork addressed her own pattern of compensatory behavior in trying to get the emotional sustenance she needed. It was not a matter of overcoming her past. It was redeeming it, allowing deep healing to take place.

Scott had his own childhood wounds from losing his father to divorce when he was still young. It was the sabbatical experience of attending the Leanne Payne conference, and reading her writing about "the injured masculine" afterward, that enabled Scott to access the broken places in his own life. In addition, family life in marriage served as a powerful impetus to examine those wounds afresh and receive healing.

These transformative changes prepared Scott and Louise for taking on a leadership role in Living Waters, a program that probes deeply into the formative influences and wounds beneath relational brokenness that need healing. Because they recognized their own wounds, they could sensitively discern others' pain.

Over the years, Louise honed her gift of accompanying people in "Listening Prayer." More than any other facet of our program, this introduces participants to intimacy with God experientially. It is not talking *about* prayer; it is sitting in God's presence and listening with another person. After actually experiencing this with Louise over a period of weeks, they can begin to apply what they have learned apart from the session. Frequently a participant will come in and exclaim, "Now I'm doing this at home on my own!"

Don finds his own way inward through the lens of art. He brings to the table insights and perspectives that are close to the mystical. All of us see our creative endeavors—places where we work with our unbridled imaginations—as integral to our approach to the mystery of the inner life of the soul.

Our personal histories make it clear why the psychological dimension is interwoven in our vocational process with individuals and in the Threshold group program. It is part of the way we think. But only part. As we companion others in Spiritual Direction, another orientation that I have come to call contemplative undergirds everything else. It is what drew me to a different kind of inner exploration and seemed to require more silence and waiting, less telling and teaching.

The term "contemplative" gets tossed around abstractly. I myself thought of it as something "monkish" and related to silence and solitude. While this attracted me on one level, I knew I was not called to live a life apart in a cloister. I belonged in "the active life," as Parker Palmer describes his own discernment of calling.[26]

In 2004, I attended a conference for spiritual leaders in the Northeast sponsored by the Shalem Institute for Spiritual Formation.[27] I became part of a small group of seven women, and over the course of five days, we were introduced to the contemplative orientation to spiritual guidance for which Shalem is known. It was refreshing to simplify my understanding of contemplation as "being present to a loving God in the moment."

Our group bonded so strongly that we decided to continue after the conference was over. We have met ever since, beginning another deep process of change within me. I learned to listen to God in silence with others, not produce clever responses to needs expressed or try to fix things, but rather sit quietly and listen for God's wisdom. It challenged much of my psychological approach that wants to take away pain and make things better. I wanted to immerse myself in a more contemplative way of being with others but knew I needed help.

Taking on the full mantle of leadership was a gradual process for Scott and Louise, requiring time to find a new comfort zone that fit for them. After a year or two, they began taking initiative in framing the shape of Life/Work Direction according to their vision in concert with ours. Don and I began to consider our future and how our roles might change.

In March, 2007, I took a weeklong retreat. When I came home, Don and I visited a favorite walking spot around the lake on Wellesley College campus to talk about our future. Don was more self-assured than I, eager to devote himself to his poetry fulltime. Then he turned to me. "What will you do?" Time stood still as I stopped and listened to my heart. The fruit of my week of silence produced a ready answer I had not explicitly framed yet. I suddenly knew and spoke with conviction: "I'm going to apply for the Shalem Program in Spiritual Guidance."

My two years in the Shalem program changed the way I sat with people who came to me for Spiritual Companionship. It knit me together with the deep prayerfulness I have always sensed when I am with Scott and Louise. It changed my marriage too and continues to transform it as I live out my life with this poet who is passionate about words, but who also claims that silence is his first language.

After completing the Shalem Program in Spiritual Guidance, I knew it was time to begin writing the story of Life/Work Direction, a project on my mind for years. As I started poring over the archives, reading old documents, and reliving old memories, I felt myself letting go—inch by inch—of my position in the creation of the work. With each page, each chapter, I was laying something down, something that had the stamp of my peculiar character on it. Simultaneously, I began noticing how Scott and Louise were picking up parts of the work with a new sense of ownership and intention. I was free to entrust the weaving of the work into someone else's hands.

In some ways Don and I, together with Dick at first, had been our own support. We had not relied on others very much. The Walkers were different in temperament and in life situation. They were more communally oriented, and gifted in particular ways of being with the new generation arising. They looked to others to hold the organizational framework; so far Don and I had provided that for them. This would likely change our long-held concept of the board.

OUR CONCEPT OF A BOARD

We were navigating a major transition beginning in 2005. We took a new look at the role of the board. A little history of our concept of board functioning is enlightening. When we incorporated in 1981, we had resisted institutionalizing, naming just the three of us on staff as board members. My previous history with boards in two nonprofit organizations made me cautious about the constraints that can throttle energy in a young movement or misdirect it as it grows. I wanted to be able to entrust the decisions that affected the work to a body that grasped the principles of our philosophy. I had been burned in my experience with a board that had become divorced from the organic sense of the ongoing mission of the work and from trends in the rapidly changing culture and had made decisions that skewed the course the staff had embraced.

I had also seen the unwieldiness of a larger and overactive board that had difficulty coming to the required consensus for action. Better to stay stripped down to the three of us at the beginning. In that way, we would not be giving over authority or control to persons who had no concept of the ministry to which we were called and was in its formative stages, or to persons who had little understanding of the unique and unorthodox way toward which we were drawn. Our resources were minimal, just three persons and a rented space for our program. We had no sponsoring group, no long-term plans for program or promotion, and no fundraising plan beyond our annual budget.

So we went our way adhering to a minimalist standard regarding board functioning. We applied for tax exemption status and were legally required by the Commonwealth to send an annual report, pay a fee, and supply the date of our "annual meeting." We followed these requirements to the letter.

The move to Jamaica Plain in 1990 had propelled us into larger thinking about our existence in the present and the future. In 1991, we asked John and Carmel Cuyler to join our board of three. We had a long history with Carmel since the inception of Life/Work Direction and we recognized her special gifts of insight and wisdom and John's complementary gifts. Carmel told us, "Coming on Board was a natural progression of my involvement with Life/Work Direction."

Two years later, our ties with Carmel were deepened when we invited her to join our staff on a part-time basis. She finished her Masters Degree in Social Work and was beginning her practice as a therapist. I said to her, "You can see people we refer to you. You can see them here." It was not a stretch for us to incorporate her services as an adjunct to our program. This began a seven-year association with Carmel, who one day a week occupied our Poustinia room as staff therapist.

Carmel says of that period of time: "This put me in a unique place in the organization, inside the staff group, but also still outside, since I lived the rest of my life apart." As for us, we were delighted to be able to refer our own people to someone of Carmel's caliber, and also someone who understood our philosophy and approach. She continued on our board, now as a de facto member by virtue of her staff relationship.

Later that year, John was called to a pastorate in Storrs, Connecticut. When the family moved, Carmel commuted one day a week to Boston. This meant weekly lunch conversations with Don and me, strengthening the mutual bonds of collegiality, a comfortable and familiar triad. Carmel found it helpful to process her work with us, and we received valuable input from her about the form and content of our work. We counted on each other for understanding, coupled with insight. I asked Carmel to describe her role as a board member in those years:

2003 Board meeting in Cuyler home. Standing: Carmel Cuyler. Seated: Eunice Schatz, John Ustach, Don Schatz

> My role is always as a responder. Eunice would prepare a report or a proposal and want feedback. But my help occurs in the context of the ministry, and my opinion is offered in response to what they propose. It flows out of the interaction. I don't walk into a board meeting with an agenda.

Carmel's contribution to our deliberations is to give ideas form, putting them into words. She asks questions that help us look at our situation with greater objectivity. Her questions might make us feel uncomfortable, yet they reassure us that we are grappling with what really matters. It is rare to have that mingling of sympathetic understanding and critical thinking. Her voice in the shaping of Life/Work Direction has been of inestimable and enduring value. Many people would not know it, for it is hidden, but her mark is there in her particular paw print on our discussions year after year.

At no time was Carmel's kind of vision more important than in 2005 when Threshold was joining Life/Work Direction. Because she remained over a long period of time, her observations helped us chronicle our development—noting what was changing and what endured as a hallmark of the particular character of our work. When the merger precipitated a fresh discussion on the place of the board, Carmel's input was especially salient:

The 2005 merger with Threshold naturally raised questions about the roles and functions of the board. Would it require a shift in function, from supporting two people in fulfilling their ministry, to thinking more organizationally as four people and two separate programs that would come together in one ministry?

As a board member, the organizational aspect of the merger was not self-evident; the organic aspect of these four people and their callings seemed obvious. I saw that Scott and Louise's life, their work and their faith, resonated with Don and Eunice, though the Walkers' experience in FOCUS and in developing Threshold was different in some ways. I saw Eunice and Don were able to support Scott and Louise in doing something distinct from what they did. I trusted these four persons and the quality of what is there.

And so we proceeded, trusting that the organizational framework would emerge in a way that supported the work.

Characteristically, most of our board discussions had been substantive—relating to philosophy and purpose—and this became even more important as we merged with Threshold. Rather than thinking of the Board in the traditional way, we thought of it as a core of persons (representatives of a larger group) who are in accord with a common purpose and philosophy—the foundation and cornerstone of what we are about and why. This often meant returning to the simple statement in our charter of incorporation. In 2005, we amplified the statement with a description of its implications for our program that would embrace the new initiatives the Walkers were bringing. It also subtly addressed our concerns about language and our spiritual roots:

To provide spiritual direction through an ecumenical context rooted in the historical Judeo-Christian tradition for persons wishing to integrate their faith with their whole life/work.

To provide spiritual direction...

Whether in the front room—in a somewhat formal vocational process, or in the back—in an intimate informal interaction, all of us are seeking ways to bring the participant's attention to God in relation to that person's life.

...through an ecumenical context

Life/Work Direction is not an arm of a church, nor does it substitute for the church. It intentionally works on the margins of many faith traditions in order to focus on the matter of prime importance, i.e., the person's relationship to God.

...in the historical Judeo-Christian tradition
We can speak only from our own faith experience, which is found in God's covenant with humankind, especially channeled through the descendants of Abraham and finally through Christ, born of a Jew. When we work with persons seeking through Eastern traditions, or without any faith, with respect we bear witness to what we know even as we are sounding the depths of the other's experience.

...for persons wanting to integrate their faith with their whole life/work.
Faith is not an "add-on" blessing, but integral to the process of discovery of one's life and work meaning. We are not vocational counselors with a spiritual dimension; our faith is inextricable from what we say and do. There is no special language we need to employ to reassure participants that we are spiritually based. Every part of our dealings with a person is fraught with the aroma of our own walk with God.

Thirty years after its inception, we continue to marvel that this simple statement of purpose stands the test of time—including changes in society, the passing of generations, and the maturing of the work in its fullness and complexity.

As it turned out, Scott and Louise also wanted to continue with a board that functioned primarily as team members, not big funders. We acknowledged that a board can have an important role and boards have power, but all of us wanted the board of the future to emerge slowly in order to be rooted spiritually. We talked about wanting board members who "got it," meaning that they grasped our marginal stance in relationship to the culture, our deeply rooted spiritual goals, and our underlying philosophy.

There were other additions to the board over time. Scott and Louise had been part of the Board for a few years in the 1990s, and Jan Curtis served for a year in the mid-1990s before suffering a debilitating stroke. John Ustach came down faithfully from his home in Maine in the years when board meetings were held in the Cuyler's home in Connecticut.

In 2005, it was natural to invite Peter and Stephanie Smith Choo to join the board. Stephanie knew Life/Work from its beginnings. She had been instrumental in encouraging the Walkers to explore a vision for what became Threshold in 1998, and had participated on staff in their program for the first five years. Peter had gone through the vocational process with Don and me in 2005, and brought a new perspective to the board in keeping with changes in his and Stephanie's lives. They married in 2005, each in their late 40s and each for the first time. There was much change afoot as Life/Work Direction and Threshold were becoming one, and a new board configuration with a newly married couple was fitting.

After 2006, we were three couples on the board—the Schatzes, the Walkers, and the Choos—a group with long associations with each other. We wait with curiosity to see how this board will cross another threshold and perceive its nature and functions differently or if past patterns will predominate. The choice is emerging as I write this story, making the decision more conscious. It may be significant that we chose to open our arms to another couple joining the board in the spring of 2010, Doug and Tracy Bennett, both recent alumni of the Threshold program. The timing for this infusion of new vigor of a younger generation feels right.

CHAPTER 13

The Tapestry:
creation of the master weaver

2010

After five years of intertwining threads, we are beginning to catch glimpses of the pattern of God's weaving. It is a colorful blend, a veritable rainbow.

Consider Don, whose very physical presence among us was striking, and who could claim the "outsider" designation, that all of us espoused in some measure, but he with more authenticity. His primary identification was as an artist, a word he filled with layers of meaning derived from his lifelong preoccupation with all the visual and aural arts, but especially music, painting, and poetry. His sense of ethnic Jewishness, influenced by his early exposure to images of the Holocaust, together with his conversion to Christianity at the time of our marriage, gave his involvement a particular twist.

How shall I describe him? His questions always probed to the underlying unspoken current. His purpose was to make the deeper point, clear away the debris of superficial thought and get to the nub of the matter. He was also interested in the way a person's experience intersected with history and culture — the larger world. He abhorred categorical thinking; he did not want to be hemmed in by constraints, especially in his thinking. He might state an opinion with authority; then in the process of discussion do a one hundred and eighty degree reversal of stance with equal power. Freedom meant freedom to change one's mind, not hold rigidly to one way of thinking.

Don's remarks often appeared to be side trails off the main path. As

Top left: Eunice waiting in her Poustinia. Top right: Don welcoming participants at the door.

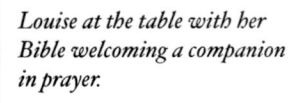

Louise at the table with her Bible welcoming a companion in prayer.

Scott in our work space ready to listen and share.

one participant who loves mountain hiking commented, "Don is one of those 'blue blazer' markers taking the traveler out of the way, or even to an entirely different destination. I can feel sidetracked, but eventually I let go of my preconceptions of the destination. If I follow Don on his circuitous path, I find that I arrive at an astonishing place I would have otherwise missed. It took me time to learn that Don's verbal meanderings were absolutely trustable."

Don says he likes "exploding peoples' logjams" by throwing in an "offbeat, an accent, a percussive note." I tended to be the one to set the rhythm. I might set up an opening, then Don would break into the musical flow of my approach and bring in a surprise. He saw how people hypnotized themselves into believing their own narrative, which had become stale. He came in with a question that made them rethink their assumptions.

Yet in daily encounters, he focused on the practical needs like scheduling, security of locked doors, the thermostat setting, the provision of tea and hot water, chair arrangement, and above all, what went on the wall and bookcases—artifacts and photographs. He was totally and immediately present to the moment when a person entered the space. He often started a conversation at the door as though they were in a continuing dialogue, for he always remembered with precision what they had said the last time we met—even if that time were months or even years before.

Don was a force to be reckoned with, but he was easily matched when Louise entered the picture like a multi-colored bird on the wing, swooping in from upstairs through the front door a minute or two late, coffee cup in hand, and instantly and totally interruptible by the concerns of whoever was standing in the entryway. I have learned to watch to see the colors she chooses to adorn herself with, and that endless array of bold and creative statements made with an unusual shawl, or exotically designed skirt—whatever the combination is, it makes its statement. "And it came from the thrift store!" she crows, for she has become adept at ferreting out the hidden treasures lurking in those aisles, and she loves being able to clothe herself with bargains!

It is Louise's visceral use of language that quickly marks her. Her sentences are rich with metaphor and image. Initially the meaning may seem obscure, but she fleshes it out with passion. She delights in ambiguity, taking a stray word and seeing it in its multiple possible meanings. Often in introducing herself she quotes the psalmist's words, "We are fearfully and wonderfully made; that my soul knows full well." "Full well!" she exclaims. "I am a full well." It is an apt phrase, for Louise is all flame within, and when she speaks from her heart, there is an eruptive quality to her words coming from the well of the Spirit that is both water and fire.

She calls her work with people "Listening Prayer," sessions animated by laughter and tears. She may sit, writing in her note pad all the while; or she may stand beside the person, hand on her shoulder addressing Jesus; or she may choose to kneel on the floor, a companion in experience and listening. For she is not just the counselor who listens; the two of them are listening together. She is unafraid of another's pain. She has known enough of it in her own life journey to empathize and to trust a way through because of the myriad ways in which Christ is present in the midst of suffering.

She can be quiet, but if for too long, the words pile up and the flow of image after image may inundate, needing expression. The daily writing of her "Morning Pages" as suggested by Julia Cameron in *The Artist's Way*,[28] captures a lot of that flow within her for later release as appropriate. Underneath, through the quiet, Louise is able to see the whole of the matter, and see it truly. Her prayers for others, spoken toward the end of a session, are trenchant and original—in the sense of being prayed through her—and leave a mark.

༄

Scott is the one of the four of us who best understands the value of taking time to bring anything he touches to wholeness and beauty—whether it be building a bunk bed desk arrangement for his son, crafting a birch bark sculpture for his stairway wall, devising an exercise for retreatants to excite their imagination, or playing with words to write a newsletter.

Some of Scott's happiest moments are spent in planning creative teaching moments for groups. He has become expert in creating simulation games that engage others so thoroughly in the activity that they momentarily forget that they are learning. These events are reminiscent of Scott's childhood years, when he played out imaginary scenarios with his three brothers in the woods near his home.

He likes order, thrives on it, and has thrown his lot in with the three of us who constantly toss grenades into the midst of his idealized sensibilities. He also wants time—lots of it—for his deliberations about a project before he can execute it according to his vision. This makes it possible for him to stop and listen closely to people before he injects the well-thought out question that turns their musings into a new and fruitful channel. Scott really hears people, and stands out among us as the person who does so without coming up with an instantaneous response. Rather, he cocks his head to one side and pauses. Then he takes the person deeper, because his question comes from another angle. I have discovered that he always has time for people. His reflective exterior is not cold and aloof. He seems to welcome interruption. Around him, I have the sense of leisure—and it is contagious.

Sometimes the laid-back way sabotages him, and he loses an object that somehow got mislaid or forgotten. If he suffers frustration from these occasions, he never shows it. Perhaps he sees that the rest of us make up for it in our over-concern and fear.

It is easy to like working with Scott because he is team-oriented, and it feeds him to have others around who have ideas, who spout them freely and with ragged edges. He takes it all in and processes it. You have to ask him— at leisure—to get the fruit of that processing. That makes him a person who is contained. The rest of us count on the solidness of that containment.

☙

Slowly, a grace-filled movement has knit our hearts together. We have let the unity arise organically, cherishing the differences. It has been an exquisite dance, embracing one another as we learned from each other, alternately leading or following as the music seemed to indicate, leaving room for unusual turns and idiosyncratic slides without losing the rhythm. It began feeling effortless over time, because we were well-conditioned by the work we do with others to support one another's "deep gladness." We are aware that our strength—individually and as a corpus—conceals the fragility underneath. This throws all of us onto the mercy of God, for "we hold this treasure in jars of clay."

☙

By 2010, Scott and Louise were comfortable taking over the reins of the program completely. I have slipped into a background role caring for certain administrative functions, while continuing with my work in Spiritual Companionship. Occasionally, the Walkers invite me to join them in the vocational process, teaching the Enneagram.

Don began calling himself "Poet-in-Residence" beginning in 2007, and devoted himself full time to his writing. He officially retired in 2010.

He marked the occasion by publishing his entire opus as a poet, delighted that modern technology (which he refuses to learn himself) could scan his thousands of pages of handwritten work onto a single disk. He refers to it as his "pancake" and enjoys distributing copies to friends and colleagues. It is his testimony. He made a typically cryptic announcement of the release of his work:

> *I've published to show bits and pieces of a movement from Good Friday to Easter. To tell of a time before and after my conversion. From Europe to America. From Death to Life...I will go on. Thanks be to God.*

It is too soon to predict what this step means either for Don, for our marriage, or for Life/Work Direction. Because we live in the house, I watch Don continue his routine of preparing the hot water for tea, checking the thermostat, and readying the space for the day's influx of participants. He rustles about among all three of us, encouraging, asking interested questions, making sure to keep in touch with the life and work going on. As for board participation, he says "no" for now. "I'll be an Advisor, like Carmel and John," he said. The rest of us know his advice is worth listening to.

I come to the end of my story, not the end of Life/Work Direction's story. It is time to acknowledge the presence of the Master Weaver in whose hands the future of this tapestry is held. With the Psalmist, I say:

> *Wonderful are your works; that I know very well.*
> *My frame*—and I dare to add, Life/Work Direction's—*was not hidden from you when it was being made in secret, intricately woven in the depths of the earth.*
> Psalm 139:14,15

Some of us thought we were at the loom, and may have imagined ourselves alone. But we were accompanied, and the over-all design was of God. Such a work cannot be expressed in the usual language—"God guided us," "we followed instructions," "God did this part and we did ours." Weaving requires a more intimate process than that. It depends on choices—of color, weight, and texture. The beauty of the design is as important as its form and usefulness. We worked a little blindly at times, seeing only the back side where the endings and beginnings of the threads were obvious. We proceeded in faith, trusting God's mastery of the intricate process of blending the colors into a wonderful work. Suffice it to say, the frame was known to God, who oversaw the weaving, his hand on ours as we worked the loom.

In gratitude and humility, I return to our sense at the founding, that "it is by God's mercy that we are engaged in this ministry." And by God's mercy it continues as long as God's mercy endures. This is when I sing the words of the loved hymn: "There's a wideness in God's mercy, wider than the sea."

That is mercy enough for us. For now, and for the future.

Epilogue

THE DOORS TO THE COMMON ROOM SWING OPEN revealing a cluster of young people beginning to rise from their places, pick up their backpacks and laptops and cell phones. It is the end of a Threshold group meeting, and the soft chatter of voices reverberates in the foyer after the deep quiet of the closing prayer.

Some of them remain sprawled on the couch and chairs, chatting with each other, reluctant to leave, beginning a conversation that will spill over into the car ride home.

One person lingers in the kitchen to ask a searching question and to receive one more benediction of prayer.

The last persons move slowly to the door. A peal of laughter breaks out in response to Louise's joking remark in parting.

We begin wheeling chairs back to their places in the workroom and office. A glance at the calendar schedule on the office wall confirms the start time for the following day.

We sink into the chairs for a moment of reverie. Three lines from *The Celtic Wheel of the Year*[29] serve as coda for the day, and for our life work.

> May we know that the texture of the journey
> is shot through with your mercy.
> Weaving Spirit, fold me in as I take my rest this night.

End Notes

1. Frederick Buechner, *Wishful Thinking: A Seekers' ABC,* p. 119.

2. Tess Ward, *Celtic Wheel of the Year,* p. 237.
   Tess Ward has written a book of heart-stopping daily prayers that creatively incorporate the Christian seasons with the Solstices and Equinoxes. The examples cited here are typical of the author's sensitivity to insights that speak to a broad range of readers.

3. William Bridges, *Transitions: Making Sense Out of Life's Changes,* pp. 90-110.

4. Richard N. Bolles, *What Color is Your Parachute? A Practical Manual for Job Hunters and Career Changers.*

5. Eunice Russell Schatz, *Still Woman Moving: A Lifetime of Change.*

6. *Ora et labora* ("pray and work") is the motto prescribed by the monastic Rule of Saint Benedict written by St. Benedict of Nursia for monks living communally under the authority of an abbot.

   Esther DeWaal, *The Way of Simplicity,* p. 76.
   "*Work and prayer flowing one into another, body and soul joined harmoniously—here is the healing unity of the whole of one's person.*"

7. Brother Lawrence of the Resurrection, *The Practice of the Presence of God.* Brother Lawrence is well known for praying all day long as he worked in the kitchen, practicing the presence of God.

8   Eunice Russell Schatz, *The Slender Thread: Stories of Pioneer Girls' First Twenty-Five Years*, p. 28.

9   Thomas Merton, *New Seeds of Contemplation*, p. 7 and pp. 32-36. Merton uses the concept of the true self and false self in a way that illuminates the connection between the psychological and spiritual. *"The superficial, external self...this 'I,' is not our real self. It is our 'individuality' and our 'empirical self' but it is not truly the hidden and mysterious person in whom we subsist before the eyes of God. The 'I' that works in the world, thinks about itself, observes its own reactions and talks about itself, is not the true 'I' that has been united to God in Christ. [We] work together with God in the creation of our own life, our own identity, our own destiny...I came into the world with a false self,...[which is the person] I want myself to be,....the one who wants to exist outside the reach of God's will and God's love...The only way I can be myself is...to discover myself in discovering God. If I find Him I will find myself and if I find my true self, I will find Him. [But] if I am left to myself [to find myself in God], it will be utterly impossible...The only One Who can teach me to find God is God, Himself, Alone."*

10 Renee Levine, *How to Get a Job in Boston (and anywhere else)*.

11 Thomas Merton, *New Seeds of Contemplation*, pp. 32-36.

12 Jacques Pasquier, "Experience and Conversion" in *The Way*, April 1977, Vol. 17, No. 2.
    "We are not converted once in our lives, but many times; and this endless series of large and small conversions, inner revolutions, leads to our transformation in Christ." Letter from Thomas Merton published in *Information Catholiques Internationales*, April, 1973, back cover.

13 Richard Rohr, *The Naked Now: Learning to See as the Mystics*, p. 88.

14 *Church Life*, Vol. II, X, January 1983, pp. 2, 16.

15 The Society of St. John the Evangelist is an Anglo-Episcopal order of monks established in England in 1866. The order established a mission in the U. S. in 1870, which by 1914 gained its autonomy from England. Its monastery is in Cambridge, MA, and Emery House for retreats in West Newbury, MA.

16 Eugene Gendlin, *Focusing*.
    While professor at the University of Chicago in the 1960s and following, Gendlin did research that identified an array of focusing skills that marked those persons who derived greatest benefit from their therapy. I was in one of his first student-initiated groups that practiced those skills together. Focusing refers to a "felt sense" in the body that gives clues to deeper emotions, and triggers memories that unleash insights into more fundamental causes of dysfunctional attitudes and behaviors and point the way to possible solutions naturally available to the client.

17 Catherine deHueck Doherty, *Poustinia: Christian Spirituality of the East for Western Man*.

18 Robert Johnson, *Owning Your Own Shadow*, pp. 97-118.

19 The Enneagram can be explored online, and through books written by these authors: Helen Palmer, *The Enneagram*; Don Riso and Russ Hudson, *Discovering the Enneagram*; Richard Rohr, *Discover the Enneagram*; Sandra Maitri, *The Spiritual Dimension of the Enneagram*; and others.

20 Elinor Shea, "A Spiritual Direction and Social Consciousness," in *The Way*. Shea brings social justice and individual spirituality together by suggesting a way of analyzing one's experience within a ministry. First we look at our concrete experience, follow with an objective social analysis based on facts and interconnections, then proceed to reflect in the light of Scripture, and end with appropriate action in the ministry based on all this.

21 Adolf Guggenbühl-Craig, *Power of the Helping Professions*, p. 15 and ff.

22 Parker Palmer, *Let Your Life Speak*.
    Palmer articulates a philosophy of vocation that coincides with the way Life/Work Direction conceptualizes calling.

23 Rohr, *The Naked Now*, p. 132.

24 Alfred Krass, "Maybe the Problem is in our Heads," *The Other Side*, May, 1980.

25 Thomas Merton, *New Seeds of Contemplation,* pp. 32-36.

26 Parker Palmer, *The Active Life.*

27 Shalem Institute for Spiritual Formation, an ecumenical Christian organization calling the people of God to deeper spiritual life for the world. It offers programs for Spiritual Guidance, Personal Spiritual Deepening, Clergy Spiritual Life and Leadership, and Leading Contemplative Prayer Groups and Retreats. In all of these, the purpose is to encourage and strengthen a contemplative orientation.

28 Julia Cameron, *The Artist's Way: A Spiritual Path to Higher Creativity.* Many persons have adopted her suggested practice of writing three pages daily as a way to unleash spontaneous creativity, and to access inner spiritual resources.

29 Tess Ward, *The Celtic Wheel of the Year,* p. 242.

Bibliographic Resources

Bolles, Richard N., *What Color is Your Parachute? A Practical Manual for Job Hunters and Career Changers.* Berkeley, CA: Ten Speed Press. Published annually.

---- and Crystal, John C., *Where Do I Go From Here With My Life?* Berkeley, CA: Ten Speed Press.

Bridges, William, *Transitions: Making Sense Out of Life's Changes.* Reading, MA: Perseus Books, 1980.

Bronson, Po, *What Should I Do With My Life?* New York: Random House, 2002.

Brother Lawrence of the Resurrection, *The Practice of the Presence of God.* Washington, D. C.: ICS Publications, 1994.

Buechner, Frederick, *Wishful Thinking: A Seekers' ABC.* San Francisco: HarperSan Francisco, 1993.

Cameron, Julia, *The Artist's Way: A Spiritual Path to Higher Creativity.* New York: Jeremy P. Tarcher/Putnam, 1992.

DeWaal, Esther, *The Way of Simplicity.* Maryknoll, NY: Orbis Books, 1998.

deHueck Doherty, Catherine, *Poustinia: Christian Spirituality of the East for Western Man*. Notre Dame, Indiana: Ave Maria Press, 1975.

Gendlin, Eugene, *Focusing*. New York: Everest House, 1978.

Guggenbühl-Craig, Adolf, *Power of the Helping Professions*. Dallas, Texas: Spring Publications, 1971.

Johnson, Robert, *Owning Your Own Shadow*. San Francisco: HarperSanFrancisco, 1991.

Levine, Renée, *How to Get a Job in Boston (and anywhere else)*. Chester, CT: Globe Pequot Press, c. 1979.

Maitri, Sandra, *The Spiritual Dimension of the Enneagram*. New York: Tarcher/Putnam, 2000.

Merton, Thomas, *New Seeds of Contemplation*. New York: New Directions, 2007 edition.

-----*The New Man*. New York: Farrar, Strauss and Giroux, 1961.

O'Connor, Elizabeth, *Journey Inward, Journey Outward*. New York: Harper & Row, 1968.

Palmer, Helen, *The Enneagram*. San Francisco: Harper SanFrancisco, 1988.

Palmer, Parker, *Let Your Life Speak: Listening for the Voice of Vocation*. San Francisco, CA: Jossey Bass, Inc., 2000.

-----*The Active Life*. San Francisco, CA: Jossey-Bass, 1990.

Pasquier, Jacques, "Experience and Conversion" in *The Way,* April 1977, Vol. 17, No. 2.

Riso, Don Richard, and Hudson, Russ, *The Wisdom of the Enneagram*. New York: Bantam Books, 1999.

Rohr, Richard, *The Naked Now: Learning to See as the Mystics See*. New York: Crossroad Publishing, 2009.

----- and Ebert, Andreas. *Discovering the Enneagram.* New York: Crossroad Publishing Co., 1991.

----- *Enneagram II: Advancing Spiritual Discernment.* New York: Crossroad Publishing, 1995.

Schatz, Eunice Russell, *The Slender Thread: Stories of Pioneer Girls' First Twenty-Five Years.* Muktileo, WA: WinePress Publishing, 1996.

----- *Still Woman Moving: A Lifetime of Change.* Xulon Press, 2002.

Shea, Elinor, "A Spiritual Direction and Social Consciousness," in *The Way.* Oxford, UK.

Ward, Tess, *The Celtic Wheel of the Year.* Winchester, UK: O Books, 2007.

Acknowledgments

Two persons constantly came to mind as I wrote this book—my tutors in organizational formation. First was Louise Troup, one of the originators of Pioneer Girls, an organization to which I refer in my story. Louise and I have talked endlessly over the last seven decades about the thorny issues confronting organizational creators and executives, drawing not only on our mutual experience in Pioneer Girls, but also on her seven years as part of a mission team in South Africa where she founded a school of nursing. At age ninety, Louise continues to have relevant insights.

The second was Phyllis Cunningham, with whom I shared staff experience first in Pioneer Girls, but even more significantly, collaboration in the reshaping of the Urban Life Center. The Center was founded in 1970, and "foundered" two years later in 1972. It was Phyllis who also saw the potential, made a decisive move involving personal sacrifice, and rescued the enterprise from crashing on the rocks. Primarily because of Phyllis, the organization survived and then thrived; it is still making its mark on Chicago today.

When I come to Life/Work Direction, I have chosen to especially acknowledge in the text the persons who were so key in the early years—Scott Walker, Stephanie Smith Choo and Carmel Franciscovich Cuyler. These three persons seemed to understand at a deep heart level the path Don and Dick and I chose to walk, and apparently felt called to stand with us. When Louise Walker came alongside her husband and moved into a central role, it was clear that her voice would become a major force in shaping the future. I also cherish the way the other two life partners—John Cuyler and Peter Choo— have humbly and faithfully entered into our developmental process in ways particular to their callings and gifts.

Four persons came on board to help me take my initial idea of writing this story into final form. Judith Carpenter, a poet and co-creator of a women's retreat center, gave me general suggestions at the beginning. Carolyn Metzler, weaver, writer, and Episcopal priest, co-labored with me through the editing process. I relied on Emily Newburger, a former participant in Life/Work Direction, to wade through the manuscript to detect errors and clean up my grammar and awkward phrasing. It is to Alicia Pritt, web and print designer and part-time farmer, that I owe deep gratitude for the artistic decisions that resulted in the appearance of the text and cover. As my project manager, she skillfully shepherded the work through the rocky shoals encountered on the way to final production. For a final proofreading, I relied on Barbara MacLean, long-standing friend and Life/Work Direction participant. What remains after all this help from others is my sole responsibility.

Throughout the entire year of this work, Don Schatz, poet and helpmate, said not one discouraging word, but rather picked me up when I was down, steered me to practical courses of action when I flailed about in uncertainty, praised my efforts, made sure I had the space and time I needed, and helped keep me true to what was of eternal importance.

I often had to bathe this project in prayer in order to keep centered. To God I give sincere and heartfelt thanks.

Eunice Russell Schatz
Life/Work Direction
32 Halifax Street
Jamaica Plain, MA 02130
617.522.5881
info@lifeworkdirection.org

LaVergne, TN USA
23 February 2011
217725LV00003B/6/P